(Use of force field analysis)

Top Issues

1) Board disorientation/

2) Cultural depression /Staff turnover,

" Culture is the organization what personality is to the individual— a hidden yet unifying theme that provides direction, meaning, + mobilization" p 63

Inconsistent treatment of personnel leads to cultural depression

"If left alone, all cultures eventually become dysfunctional" p. 65

- Regular all staff meetings for sharing vision/mission/status
- staff adv committee to inform mgt
- Clear artic + refreshing of values/v/m
- Staff satif surveys + recognition program

) Political Performance /self serving agendas

- Happens when power is concentrated in the wrong hands
- gain an understanding of the rules that make them dependent or susceptible

) Role confusion: Board /Exec Dir

inner/outer circle facil. strategy p102

3) Financial misfortune

- ignoring the elephant in the room
- info overload
- intentional + unintentional filtering of info

safe environ w/ clear structure

(6) fundphobia
　　> invite the right person to make a
　　fin. gift

Other Jossey-Bass Leadership and Management Titles:

Forging Nonprofit Alliances, *Jane Arsenault*

Creating Your Employee Handbook, *The Management Center, Leyna Bernstein, author*

The Drucker Foundation Self-Assessment Tool for Nonprofit Organizations, Revised Edition, *The Peter F. Drucker Foundation for Nonprofit Management*

Strategic Planning for Public and Nonprofit Organizations, *John M. Bryson*

Marketing Nonprofit Programs and Services, *Douglas B. Herron*

The Jossey-Bass Guide to Strategic Communications for Nonprofits, *Kathleen Bonk, Henry Griggs, Emily Tynes*

The Leader of the Future, *Frances Hesselbein, Marshall Goldsmith, Richard Beckhard, editors*

The Organization of the Future, *Frances Hesselbein, Marshall Goldsmith, Richard Beckhard, editors*

The Community of the Future, *Frances Hesselbein, Marshall Goldsmith, Richard Beckhard, Richard F. Schubert, editors*

Leading Beyond the Walls, *Frances Hesselbein, Marshall Goldsmith, Iain Somerville, editors*

The Collaboration Challenge: How Nonprofits and Businesses Succeed Through Strategic Alliances, *James E. Austin*

Leader to Leader Journal

Leader to Leader: Enduring Insights on Leadership from the Drucker Foundation's Award-Winning Journal, *Frances Hesselbein, Paul Cohen, editors*

Why Nonprofits Fail

To April and Zach

Why Nonprofits Fail

Overcoming Founder's Syndrome, Fundphobia, and Other Obstacles to Success

Stephen R. Block

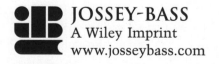

JOSSEY-BASS
A Wiley Imprint
www.josseybass.com

Published by Jossey-Bass
A Wiley Imprint
989 Market Street, San Francisco, CA 94103-1741   www.josseybass.com

Jossey-Bass books and products are available through most bookstores. To contact Jossey-Bass directly call our Customer Care Department within the U.S. at 800-956-7739, outside the U.S. at 317-572-3986, or fax 317-572-4002.

Jossey-Bass also publishes its books in a variety of electronic formats. Some content that appears in print may not be available in electronic books.

Library of Congress Cataloging-in-Publication Data
Block, Stephen R.
   Why nonprofits fail: overcoming founder's syndrome, fundphobia, and other obstacles to success/Stephen R. Block—1st ed.
      p. cm.
Includes bibilographical references and index.
   ISBN 0-7879-6409-3 (alk. paper)
1.   Nonprofit organization.—Management. I. Title.
   HD62.6.B586 2003
   658'.048—dc22
                                                        2003022254

Printed in the United States of America
FIRST EDITION
HB Printing   10 9 8 7 6 5 4 3 2

Contents

Preface

In the 1940s, a friendly possumlike swamp creature named Pogo appeared regularly in newspapers commenting wryly on politics and philosophy. Although what Pogo had to say was often funny, occasionally his wit and the simplicity of his statements carried far deeper meaning. I dare risk saying that my nonprofit organizational management philosophy is based in part on the pedagogical wisdom of a cartoon character!

In one cartoon, Pogo asks what if the one guy is right and the ten thousand is wrong. To paraphrase Pogo's question, how is it that if 10,001 individuals in an organization all experience the same events, why do 10,000 of them all behave one way but one individual behaves differently from all the rest? The answer is that the one individual reacts differently because he or she views the events through a different lens. Throughout this book, you will find references to lenses, frameworks, paradigms, and theoretical models. For our purposes, these terms are interchangeable and refer to a conceptualization process that helps us understand our experiences and brings them into focus. Like the lens in a pair of eyeglasses, if the strength is changed or if the lens is infused with a color, the objects that we see through those lenses will look different. By altering our perspective, our outlook, interpretation, and responses can also change.

The simplicity of Pogo's paradigm may hold the answers to many organizational behavior issues. It suggests that common problem-solving approaches may not always work and that we may need to use other frameworks to see problems in a different light. Alternative viewpoints may lead to uncommon interventions that surprisingly will be effective.

History has repeatedly demonstrated that the masses can be wrong in how they view the world around them. At one time, most people believed that the earth was flat. Looking at the world through a different paradigm can change one's perception and interpretation of reality. Twenty residents of Salem, Massachusetts, for example, lost their lives in 1692 because an entire community believed that they were witches and needed to be destroyed to prevent satanic evil from running rampant among the citizenry. The accusations and trials stopped when the community altered its beliefs and assumptions. When our assumptions change, so often do our beliefs in ideas that we once held to be sacred and true.

Board members, executive directors, other managers, staff, and volunteers come to their nonprofit organization with their own beliefs and attitudes reflected in the knowledge and opinions that they have stored over the years. In fact, all of these various members of nonprofit organizations come to their roles and responsibilities with their own perceptual frameworks that are intact and sometimes deeply entrenched. If an individual's framework is rigid and inflexible, he or she will view and interpret nonprofit issues and challenges in a constant and static way. The consistency of a held viewpoint does not necessarily lead to organizational stability or effectiveness. In fact, an unwillingness to explore organizational issues in alternative ways can lead to organizational turmoil, dysfunction, and ultimately organizational failure.

The desire to prevent nonprofit mission and organizational failure is what drove the creation of this book. It was written because of my intense professional interest in seeing that nonprofit organizations operate effectively. It is my hope that this book will become a helpful tool for nonprofit managers. Over the years, the ideas in this book have helped me successfully resolve persistent nonprofit organizational problems by approaching problem-solving activities in unconventional ways.

I have relied on the use of case studies to show how organizational reality is constructed through assumptions. The way one views one's organizational world may be perpetuating problems instead of helping to resolve them. One of the most constructive forms of problem solving starts by questioning one's own personal paradigms and ideas about nonprofit organizational behavior. It is my hope that readers will question the formation and persistence of the nonprofit organizational problems with which they are struggling and will experiment with more radical problem resolution strategies when they find that customary problem-solving approaches fall short of success.

Structure of the Book

The book is divided into two parts. Part I consists of four chapters written primarily to highlight the critically important role of nonprofit managers and to recognize the many challenges and concerns they face. Board members who like reading nonprofit management books will find these chapters of interest, as will students of nonprofit management. Part II, consisting of seven chapters, provides an exploration of problems and possible solutions. The Conclusion summarizes the matters discussed in Parts I and II. Instructors will find that the content of this book dovetails nicely with any text currently being used to teach courses related to nonprofit management or nonprofit organizational behavior.

Although it is more of a practitioner's book, it should be useful in the classroom in courses on nonprofit management, nonprofit organizational behavior and change, nonprofit organizational development, and strategic decision making for nonprofit managers. Since several of the problems that are covered in depth focus on the

roles and responsibilities of nonprofit boards of directors and the relationship between the board and management staff, I will be using
the book to supplement readings and for small group discussions in
my graduate course on nonprofit boards and executive leadership.

In Part I, the opening chapter, "Preventing Failure, Ensuring
Success," outlines the goals of the book. It describes the scope of
the nonprofit sector and the vital role that nonprofit managers play
in fulfilling the missions, dreams, and hopes of citizens throughout
the world.

Chapter Two, "The Need for Alternative Tools," discusses the
responsibility that nonprofit managers have to continue to challenge their beliefs and assumptions and to improve their skills and
abilities. The chapter suggests that nonprofit managers need to be
open to unique and alternative approaches to solving problems and
managing planned change efforts.

Chapter Three, "The Framework and the Steps," describes the
basic framework that is used to assess problems and to devise intervention strategies to solve problems and promote change. The
chapter explains that theories can be used as a framework or a lens
to see a problem in a different light. Viewing problems differently
permits the nonprofit manager to develop alternative problem-
solving strategies.

Chapter Four, "First-Order and Second-Order Approaches
to Change," discusses the difference between routine problem-
solving approaches and the use of alternative strategies when
routine approaches fail. The chapter explains how to classify
problems into two categories, first-order and second-order problems.
The more challenging the problem, the more likely that a second-
order approach will be required for resolving problems and effect-
ing planned change.

The chapters in Part II, Chapters Five through Eleven, cover
problems common to nearly all nonprofit organizations. Each chapter is devoted to one specific problem and is illustrated with one or
more case examples followed by an analysis of the issues, alternative ways to view the problem, and recommendations for different

intervention strategies when the routine ones fail. The case studies are based on real situations, but the names of the nonprofit organizations, geographical locations, and individuals referred to in the case examples are all fictitious.

The problems that are presented in these chapters were selected because of their universality among nonprofit organizations. Consequently, readers may have a sense of déjà vu and wonder if they are reading about their own nonprofit organization. Indeed, similarities may exist because these types of issues have been observed in nonprofit organizations throughout the United States and Canada and among nongovernmental organizations (NGOs) in industrialized nations around the world. But like winning the lottery, the chances that the case examples in the book are about your nonprofit organization are quite remote!

The seven problems covered in the book are as follows:

Chapter Five, "Recruitment Disorientation," describes the relationship between recruitment practices and problems that emerge once an individual has been voted onto the board.

Chapter Six, "Cultural Depression in Nonprofit Organizations," describes an organizational culture problem.

Chapter Seven, "Political Performance," focuses on organizational politics and its related behaviors.

Chapter Eight, "Role Confusion," describes problems that result from ambiguous roles and responsibilities of nonprofit managers and board members.

Chapter Nine, "Financial Misfortune," describes a nonprofit organization financial health problem that escalates when board members and staff avoid their financial management responsibilities.

Chapter Ten, "Fundphobia," centers on problems that emerge when board members do not want to participate in fundraising activities.

Chapter Eleven, "Founder's Syndrome," focuses on leadership and power issues that can exist when the nonprofit organization is managed by its founder. The chapter discusses two examples of escalating issues between founders and board members.

The Conclusion, " Managing Nonprofit Organizational Change," recaps the important principles addressed throughout the book. The intent is to encourage the reader to develop a framework or mind-set for effectively managing and governing nonprofit organizations. The fundamental message is that executive directors and other non-profit managers have a responsibility to see that their nonprofit organizations are effective and do not fail!

At the back of the book, I provide two helpful Resources. The first gives an overview of seven of the theories referred to through-out the book: behavioral leadership theory, personality theory, expectancy theory, Lewin's Force Field Analysis theory, communication theory, intergroup conflict theory, and decision-making theory. Readers can refer to this resource as they read the book to clarify certain points and to review the application from theory to practice. Motivated readers will also want to consult the works appearing in the second resource, a Recommended Reading list, in addition to those listed in the References.

Greenwood Village, Colorado   Stephen R. Block
October 2003

Acknowledgments

There are many individuals and organizations that I wish I could publicly thank for helping me shape my thinking and inspiring me to write this book. Without their confidence in my ideas and their willingness to try different organizational problem-solving approaches, I would not have their stories to include in this book. Unfortunately, I cannot list their individual names or organizational affiliations without breaching their anonymity.

However, there are some people whom I can openly acknowledge. I owe much to my friends and colleagues at Denver Options, without whose shared vision, determination to risk, and willingness to test boundaries, daily organizational life would be less than meaningful. In particular, I want to express my appreciation to members of my management team. Over the years, they have provided me with a source of opportunities to observe, learn, and share ideas about turning organizational theories into practice: Kathy Athens, Lee Ann Bellum, Rosemary Berry, Gayann Brandenburg, Nina Cruchon, Ted Hernandez, Nancy Hodges, Jodi Merrill-Brandt, Becky Miller, Arnie Swenson, and Lance Wheeland. Also, my appreciation goes to Nolbert Chavez for his political insight and to Richard Westfall for his legal advice. While it is not possible to list all of the board members who were supportive of my work, there are two others who played central roles: Denny O'Malley and Sean R. Gallagher were two exemplary board chairs. Cecilia McMurray provided vital day-to-day support, running interference, protecting my schedule, and helping me juggle multiple deadlines.

I appreciated the discussions with Steve Rosenberg, who played a key role in our original research on founder's syndrome. Also, I owe thanks to Kathleen Beatty, dean of the Graduate School of Public Affairs (GSPA) at the University of Colorado, Denver, for supporting a nonprofit concentration in the M.P.A. program that has given me a platform to teach and express my ideas about nonprofit organizational behavior. At GSPA, Suzanne Oliver was very diligent in her role as a graduate research assistant, tracking down source material and taking a leap of faith that I would return her borrowed books and journals to the library. I paid all of the fines!

I appreciated the helpful conversations that I had with Art Hogling, Bill Ziefle, and Ted Hernandez, who read and commented on drafts of the book. The detailed comments of three anonymous reviewers were also insightful.

This book would not have been possible without the encouragement and advice of Dorothy Hearst, senior editor at Jossey-Bass. Lots of moving parts have to come together to complete a book. So thanks are due to Allison Brunner and the other members of the Jossey-Bass nonprofit team.

I am most grateful for the ability to have my work expertly reviewed by my closest friend, colleague, and critic—my wife, April. I am deeply appreciative of her support and her helping me carve out the time for writing this book. And finally, a word of thanks to my son, Zach. Little does he know how inspiring it was for me to read his writings. It gave me the added boost to go back and write some more.

—S.R.B.

The Author

Stephen R. Block is the founding executive director of Denver Options, now in its eleventh year of managing the developmental disabilities service system in Denver, Colorado, under a private non-profit–public sector partnership. His career in nonprofit management includes twenty-four years as an executive director and five years as a clinical social worker. Previously, he served as executive director of the Denver-based Institute for Nonprofit Organization Management, providing a broad range of training and consultation to nonprofit organizations and governmental agencies throughout the United States. Before that, he was the executive director of the National Association of Social Workers' Colorado chapter. He started his career as a social worker for a local social service authority in Newcastle-upon-Tyne, England. After returning to the States, he worked for the Indiana University Medical Center and was appointed chief social worker in adult psychiatry.

Besides being a practicing manager, Block is renowned as an educator and author on nonprofit management and governance. In addition to his work at Denver Options, he is an associate research professor and director of the nonprofit management program at the University of Colorado at Denver's Graduate School of Public Affairs and a recipient of the university's Award for Excellence in Teaching. He developed and taught nonprofit management courses at Regis University's Graduate School of Professional Studies and was a visiting faculty member at San Francisco State University. He also taught courses for the University of Denver's Graduate School of Social Work, Indiana University, and Colorado State University, and he has guest-lectured at prominent universities and colleges throughout the United States.

Block's personal philosophy of sharing knowledge and his interest in helping nonprofit organizations improve are expressed in his professional writings, as evidenced by nearly four dozen publications, including books, book chapters, journal articles, and encyclopedia entries.

Block is active in his professional associations and in his local community, serving on governing and advisory boards. For two years, he hosted a weekly talk radio program focusing on health and human services. The Denver City Council adopted a formal resolution approved by the mayor to honor Block for outstanding service and contributions to the city of Denver.

Block received his bachelor of arts degree from Brooklyn College of the City University of New York. He received his master's degree in social work from the Graduate School of Social Work, Indiana University, underwritten by a grant from the National Institute of Mental Health. He was honored by Pi Alpha Alpha as the outstanding doctoral candidate in public administration and received his doctor of philosophy degree in public administration with a concentration in nonprofit organization management from the University of Colorado's Graduate School of Public Affairs.

Block lives in the Denver area with his wife, April, and their teenage son, Zachary.

Part I

Charting a New Path to Success

Part I focuses on the important responsibilities of nonprofit organizations in society and the essential role that nonprofit managers play in the success of these organizations. Achieving organizational success and avoiding organizational failure is a significant objective for the nonprofit manager. But as we see in Part I, nonprofit managers face no shortage of problems and challenges.

For those who have the responsibility of managing and governing nonprofit organizations, it may often seem that there are critical shortages of effective solutions. Part I explores the idea that any shortage of effective problem solving is a limitation of our own making. When routine problem-solving methods do not work, we have a choice: we can stay stuck, or we can restructure the way we think about the problems. Instead of being bogged down with unsuccessful solutions, Part I helps us see that by using organizational theories, it is possible to understand the obstacles and maneuver around them by charting alternative paths to organizational success.

1

Preventing Failure, Ensuring Success

Nonprofit organizations add vitality to our communities and provide essential services that enhance and protect our well-being. However, nonprofit organizations also face challenges in a society that lives with the turbulent forces of economic, social, political, and technological change. Often the nonprofit manager is the critical center to safeguard the survival of mission-oriented nonprofit entities. We depend on the nonprofit manager's ability to marshal the skills and energies needed to overcome organizational and environmental constraints to ensure accomplishment of mission-oriented services that will improve the human condition.

The performance capabilities of nonprofit managers can have a profound effect on the ability of a nonprofit organization to effectively serve its community. Nonprofit managers require skill-based and knowledge-based competencies that help them be effective technicians and masters in solving problems, implementing necessary change, and ultimately getting things done. This book is about developing the specific knowledge and skills needed to meet the challenges that inhibit positive organizational change.

It may be popular to say that organizational change is scary and that people in organizations resist change because they fear the unknown. But like it or not, change will occur. As a nonprofit manager, our goal is to ensure that organizational change occurs for the better. I share the view of organizational behavior and management experts Paul Hersey, Kenneth Blanchard, and Dewey Johnson (1996), who state that to be an organizational leader implies that you must learn to love change because it is intrinsic to the leadership process—and further that leaders must overcome their resistance to change and become change managers. Nonprofit managers must learn to control change and not let their nonprofit organization fall victim to change occurring however it will. Uncontrolled change is a consequence of nonprofit managers' inability to resolve problems effectively, whether the problems are between individuals, teams, departments, or organizations. Understandably, to control and plan for change, a nonprofit manager must have expertise as a problem solver.

My purpose in writing this book is to help the nonprofit manager acquire the tools that he or she needs to be a highly effective organizational problem solver. Simply put, if you are able to solve difficult problems and manage change rather than merely react to it, the odds of your success will increase. The approach I set forth in this book focuses on challenging and persistent problems that are very difficult to eradicate, potentially draining valuable nonprofit organizational resources. In addition, certain unrelenting common problems can cause a decision-making logjam that gets in the way of doing good things for people and communities.

What has long been needed is an approach to problem solving and change management that is both practical in application and conceptually sound. Over the years, I have prevailed over some extremely difficult nonprofit management problems using the same unconventional approaches to problem resolution and planned change that are discussed throughout this book. My closest colleagues lightheartedly suggest that my nonconforming approach to nonprofit organizational behavior and change has achieved uncanny results as a by-product of my having chutzpah mixed with some Brooklyn-born street fighter instincts and coupled with the learned skills of a fast-talking, fast-driving New York City cabbie. Although I do not downplay that my past may have something to do with my current worldview, my approach to nonprofit organizational behavior issues has more to do with being fundamentally grounded in theories of organizational behavior, communication, psychology, and applied psychotherapy. In fact, throughout this book, I draw on these and other theories to show nonprofit managers how to classify a problem, assess the problem, and determine what theoretical models might be helpful for formulating specific intervention strategies to resolve the problem and effect planned change.

If some of the strategies strike you as unconventional and new, rest assured that this solution-based approach has been twenty-five years in the making. I have been refining this approach to problem resolution and planned change throughout my years as an executive director, as a researcher, and as an educator I have had the opportunity to train and advise hundreds of nonprofit managers who needed to solve particular problems that were barriers to organizational success. By applying these unique problem-solving techniques in their organizations, they were able to solve problems, implement change, and move on to fulfill their obligations as the managers of a nonprofit organization. Some of their issues are highlighted in the case studies featured in Part Two.

It would be misleading for me to suggest that the use of these tools will guarantee success. Some variables are unpredictably difficult to control, especially when we are unable to gain the cooperation and understanding of other people. You will find one case study in this book, on Founder's Syndrome, that exemplifies such difficult human behavior. Whatever obstacles are encountered, the nonprofit manager must learn to use the approach and techniques confidently in order to disrupt dysfunctional patterns of organizational behavior. We are more likely to be successful as we become more adept at cutting through the symptoms and reaching into the heart of the problem. The more fine-tuned skills that a nonprofit manager has, the more effective he or she will be. Becoming skillful requires practice in the analysis of presenting problems. It also requires evaluating the results from the implemented problem resolution strategies that were targeted to address specific issues that were interfering with organizational change.

In many ways, the book is about enhancing nonprofit managers' opportunities for achieving organizational success and diminishing the chances of failure. Although it may sound corny, I think that nonprofit organizations have an obligation not to fail. For this reason, I believe that nonprofit managers have a duty to take some calculated risks, trying new problem-solving approaches when conventional approaches have not worked. Risk taking does not mean engaging in unethical, unlawful, or wanton behavior. It may mean going out to the edge of what feels comfortable in order to head off or overcome a failing situation.

The subject of failure and the importance of achieving nonprofit organizational success are the focal points of the rest of this chapter. I am using the remaining space to remind us of how valuable nonprofit organizations are to society and why we must continually improve our capacity to manage nonprofit organizations effectively.

In some situations, the word *failure* is used to describe severe organizational problems associated with incompetence, wrongdoing, or mismanagement. Organizations wearing these labels of ineptitude may find it nearly impossible to recover from a tainted image and may find their funding and volunteer support substantively curtailed for many years. It may even force them to go out of business.

In other situations, failure may be the result of individuals engaging in patterns of behavior that set up barriers to organizational success or obstruct processes that could lead to satisfactory problem resolution. This latter type of failure is more prevalent in organizations, and it can occur without regard to the competency levels of the organization's managers or line staff. In fact, seasoned executive directors and skilled nonprofit managers will occasionally find themselves in organizational predicaments that escalate when trying to find a satisfactory resolution. The more they try to find a way out of the problem, the worse the problem gets. These seemingly no-way-out situations are the type that can gnaw at the confidence levels of managers and cause a spiraling-downward effect. The outcome can be frustration, anger, and a demoralized staff and board of directors who feel and look like they are weakening in meeting their responsibilities. The combination of these effects becomes branded as organizational failure. When a nonprofit organization's reputation reaches this point of distress, it can have a deleterious result on the organization's programs and services.

Often there is a way out of the traps that appear to have no end. The ideas that will be introduced, described, and demonstrated in this book will provide a framework for resolving those complicated and recurring problems. By using case examples, we will be able to see how problems are perpetuated and what steps to take to assess, develop, and implement powerful change strategies that can break the patterns of organizational behavior that interfere with the advancement of an organization's nonprofit mission.

For the most part, these tools will work to your advantage and are not so extreme as to raise questions about the veracity of the intervention. However, there are times when the dynamics of an organizational problem become so highly dysfunctional that even the measures described in this book will not work. In those situations, the "fix" may be so radical that some will find the solution as objectionable as the problem it is attempting to address. Such intervention strategies are a subject for another time and place.

The degree to which a nonprofit organization is more or less effective can have a significant bearing on meeting the needs of a community. As lofty as it may sound, nonprofit organizations represent the conscience of society and are the driving force in many efforts that are aimed at improving the quality of life for citizens throughout the United States and in some cases the world. Our reliance on nonprofit organizations is pervasive and encompassing. Consider, for example, the continuum of human needs that nonprofit organizations fulfill—from a place where we adopt our dogs and cats to touring museums, zoos, and aquariums to Saturday's Little League soccer and baseball games to care of ailing family

members by visiting nurses to the spiritual comfort of worship services. Stated simply, people rely on nonprofit organizations.

Nonprofit organizations truly and immeasurably influence daily
life. Just look at some of the many benefits that nonprofits provide
to society:

- Religious expression

- Preserving cultural mores

- Advancing scientific findings

- Improving the physical and emotional health of people
  of all ages

- Offering artistic expression in the performing arts

- Educating people of all levels of intellect

- Mediating issues between citizen groups and government

- Protecting citizens from harmful corporate practices

To accomplish their goals, nonprofit organizations in the United
States rely on the generosity of financial contributors, who give
more than $212 billion annually, and the personal time and efforts
of over 109 million volunteers. The lifeblood of the nonprofit sector
depends on the ongoing support and generosity of these individuals, in addition to the financial grants issued by government, corporations, and foundations. Individual and institutional support is
likely to continue as long as nonprofit organizations remain free of
scandal, demonstrate accountability, and stay mission-directed. For
all of these reasons, it is imperative that resources be managed effectively and governed wisely.

Government has granted certain privileges to nonprofit organizations because of the recognition that nonprofits add value to society. If nonprofits operate effectively and with accountability, they

can have all of the safeguards of corporations without the obligations of paying taxes. In addition, government supports the mission-
oriented activities of nonprofit organizations by collecting
individual and corporate income taxes and then redistributing
billions of dollars through grants and contracts.

Promoting popular causes for the public good is only one of the
important roles that nonprofit organizations play. Historically, nonprofit organizations have also been associated with championing
certain objectionable views and advancing questionable values on
behalf of humanitarian efforts that society has not always appreciated or even deemed acceptable. The nonprofit sector has provided
a forum for controversial beliefs that have had only marginal
support. By giving a voice to unpopular ideas, eventually those ideas
that merit support by a larger majority often do find their way to
broader support. Prohibitions against child labor, the abolishment
of slavery, advancing civil rights, and promoting HIV research are
just a few examples of social reforms that originated by a few individuals who voluntarily associated with each other to speak out
against the prevailing viewpoints of their time. In fact, it has been
said that the impetus for every major social reform in the United
States has been sparked by voluntary action.

Besides a rich history that is rooted in centuries of religious influences and charitable practices, today's nonprofits are important economic partners of private business and governmental agencies.
Some government agencies contract with nonprofit organizations
to fulfill obligations that would otherwise be more costly if delivered by government employees. Furthermore, not only do for-profit
companies benefit from the products and services purchased by nonprofit organizations, but nonprofit research entities also provide
product testing through research and development activities.

Overall, nonprofit organizations contribute to the economic
health of the nation. Approximately one in twelve individuals is
employed in the nonprofit sector. Through employees' payments of
taxes and the routine spending of their earnings, the funds of the

nonprofit organization are channeled back into the community, thereby also bolstering the nation's economy.

In light of their indispensable role in various communities and in the economy, it is vitally important that nonprofit organizations are effectively managed, governed, and ultimately succeed. Evidently, our reliance on the skills of nonprofit managers is immeasurable, and this fact relates directly to the purpose of writing this book. My goal is to help you objectify your approach to problem solving and planned change. More specifically, I believe that the use of the techniques described in this book will help you be a more effective nonprofit manager. You will find that some of the advantages of using this alternative approach are as follows:

- The approach is easy to use and can be adapted by every nonprofit manager without disruption to one's existing management style or theoretical orientation.

- It provides the tools for evaluating and overcoming problems that can occur in any aspect of nonprofit management practice.

- It can be used to test ideas for creative problem resolution and planned change intervention strategies.

- It can help the nonprofit manager assess a problematic situation, leading to a more appropriate intervention and better outcomes for the organization.

- It relies on the use of credible theories but is essentially theory-free, not tying down the nonprofit manager to one theory.

- It is flexible in that the nonprofit manager is in control of deciding on the best theory to fit the problem.

- It relies on both facts and beliefs.

- It values the art of practice—creativity combined with mission.

- It values guidance from scientific methods by using basic tools and concepts of research in the practice arena.

2

The Need for Alternative Tools

I hope that you agree with the premise I laid out in Chapter One that nonprofit organizations can ill afford to falter on their commitments to the communities that are the beneficiaries of their goals and missions in the public interest.

I trust that we can also agree that managing a nonprofit organization is not an easy job. It can even be a daunting experience, given the complexities and responsibilities associated with managing finances and human resources, interacting with boards and the community, and having to demonstrate accountability under the watchful eyes of funders, key stakeholder groups, and regulatory agencies. Consequently, this chapter is based on the belief that organizations in the nonprofit sector are in need of sophisticated managers who have the organizational acumen and technical skills to control complex strategic issues, solve problems, and implement change.

The aim of this chapter is to confirm that it will be difficult to achieve the requisite level of expertise without having alternative approaches to solving problems and managing planned change efforts. I believe I need to demonstrate that the management tools that are most relied on—acquired by formal study or informally by the "sink or swim" method—may be technically weak or simply out of the range of what we need for handling certain difficult and persistent problems. By not using the most effective approaches to

problem resolution and planned change, we may be making difficult matters even worse.

My plea is for nonprofit managers to question their dependency
on using one approach to implementing problem resolution strategies. In no way do I want nonprofit managers to feel discontented
with the tools that work for them. Instead, I would like these managers to consider using less conventional approaches when their
ordinarily reliable tools fail.

Historically, nonprofit organizations were not concerned with
management proficiency and did not evaluate their progress or their
capacity to ensure that they had top-notch managers running programs and effectively directing day-to-day operations. In fact, management guru Peter Drucker (1989, p. 89) observed that at one time,
"management was a dirty word for those involved in nonprofit organizations. It meant business, and nonprofits prided themselves on
being free of the taint of commercialism and above such sordid considerations as the bottom line." Furthermore, management knowledge, skills, and abilities have never been prerequisites for becoming
a founder of a nonprofit organization and were not essential requirements for being hired into positions of executive director.

Often executive candidates were recruited on the basis of their
performance in nonmanagement roles. If individuals excelled in
their professional field, there was a good chance they would be
drafted into senior management roles. For example, a clinical social
worker skilled in counseling would be rewarded with an executive
director position. Similar promotional opportunities were available
for teachers, psychologists, nurses, and other outstanding employees who demonstrated their effectiveness and loyalty to an organization's programs.

Although this Peter Principle approach of placing nonmanagers
in executive management positions beyond their capacity persists,
the pool of trained and educated nonprofit managers who are pre-
sumably more qualified for the management challenges of directing

and leading nonprofit organizations has been growing. This increasing pool of potentially more competent nonprofit managers is the result of individuals completing undergraduate and graduate degree programs in nonprofit management as well as professional degree programs that offer nonprofit management studies as a concentration. Nonprofit management education has gained in popularity since its introduction into higher education in the early 1980s.

Also during the 1980s, nonprofit organizations began to feel the pinch of sweeping changes to federal policies on grant giving and contracting practices. As a result of so-called Reaganomics, nonprofit organizations found themselves vying for more local and state block grant funds and were no longer the recipients of federal dollars that had formerly seemed available just for the asking. In addition, with greater expectations being shifted to the private sector, foundations and corporate giving programs were inundated with requests for support and funding. One of the unintended consequences, which eventually proved beneficial for the nonprofit sector, was increased competition for charitable dollars. With greater demands on the funding community to sort through proposals and limit giving to a small percentage of the askers, the funders began to enforce more standards, such as taking a closer look at the efficiencies and effectiveness of the nonprofit organizations that were requesting funding support.

A new emphasis on accountability forced nonprofit boards to question whether their management staff could meet the expectations of philanthropists. As a result, nonprofit management technical assistance centers emerged along with educational programming aimed at bolstering the management skills of nonprofit organizational managers. Being able to demonstrate organizational success became a significant goal throughout the nonprofit sector.

Because nonprofit education and training programs have been in existence for a relatively short period, individuals without formal management education remain the predominant group of managers in charge of the more than one million nonprofit organizations that exist around the world. Over the years, these individuals developed their management knowledge and skills mainly through trial and error and relying on good common sense. Many of the midcareer professionals have since enrolled in nonprofit management degree and certificate programs, having recognized the potential benefits of returning to the classroom for an education that is focused on improving their nonprofit management knowledge and skills. Some want to learn the theories or principles that can help explain how or why they have been making management decisions over the years.

Besides these experienced adult learners, there are also many students enrolled in nonprofit management degree and certificate programs that have very limited management or work experience in the nonprofit sector. These individuals recognize the value-laden emphasis of nonprofit organizations and have decided that they want a career in the nonprofit sector. A degree or a certificate in nonprofit management will help them compete for management positions and help compensate for their limited years in the workplace. Given this mix of the home-schooled and the inexperienced, it seems understandable why nonprofit organizations have had the long-standing reputation of "doing good" but not the reputation of "good doers." In other words, people who "do good" have not been equated with people who are knowledgeable, skilled, or effective managers.

Although it may not be a fair or accurate picture, nonprofit organizations have been cast as organizations that often operate by crisis and chaos. One reason why nonprofits are seen in this light is that millions of Americans are approached daily for volunteer help and financial contributions. Furthermore, television news, newspaper articles, and direct mail solicitations throughout the country periodically report on nonprofit orchestras, museums, theater groups, or other types of nonprofits that may have to close their doors for lack of funding. These reports appear alongside stories of human suffering that cannot be adequately addressed because of the overwhelming demand for shelter, food, clothing, and medical care for indigent individuals and troubled families.

On the one hand, the chaos and crisis that characterize some nonprofits may result from external forces putting pressures on these organizations to do more than they possibly can. On the other hand, critics might say that it is the nonprofit managers and board members who propel organizational discord from the inside. Consider the comments of governance experts Barbara Taylor, Richard Chait, and Thomas Holland (1996), writing in the *Harvard Business Review*: "Effective governance by the board of a nonprofit organization is a rare and unnatural act. Only the most uncommon of nonprofit boards functions as it should by harnessing the collective efforts of accomplished individuals to advance the institution's mission and long-term welfare" (p. 36).

On a similar theme of concern, Brian O'Connell (1985), a well-known nonprofit sector advocate, expressed his angst over the idiosyncratic characteristics of nonprofit organizations when he noted, "People care passionately about causes or institutions and they want the best for them now, but human institutions are all less than perfect, and voluntary organizations in particular can require more interaction than most of us can bear."

Whether the vitality of a nonprofit organization faces challenges from external sources or from within, or both, we have come to expect nonprofit organizations to right the wrongs of society and prevent future mishaps. As Steve Ott (2001, p. 49) observes, "The nonprofit sector has become the object of high expectations among elected officials and a large segment of the general public." We then come back to the need for highly developed management skills among our nonprofit organizational leaders.

To advance the aim of improving nonprofit management capabilities, there has been, along with the launching of university-based educational programs, a proliferation of specialized literature in the form of books and journals. All of these knowledge-building advances have been viewed positively for the professionalization of the management role in the nonprofit sector.

With all of these academic advances, why would some nonprofit organizations—even those managed by educated and trained nonprofit managers—continue to display various forms of organizational failure? In my opinion, five components comprise the answer to that question. First, the nonprofit organizations are being judged harshly because they still carry the stigma of not being managed in a businesslike way.

Second, nonprofit organization management is still evolving as an academic discipline. Consequently, our educational programs and research efforts have not fully identified all of the combinations of competencies that are necessary to be a highly effective nonprofit manager.

Third, in areas where we have identified key competencies, the quality of instruction has been inconsistent across the country. In some institutions, the nonprofit faculty are as inexperienced in the practice of nonprofit management as some of their students who have never worked in the nonprofit sector. In other institutions, the faculty consist of adjunct instructors who have years of nonprofit management experience but may not have the instructional skills to teach and convey their practice wisdom effectively to adult learners.

Fourth, given the economic realities of budget constraints among institutions of higher education, the ability to offer the ideal curriculum and content is sometimes compromised to save money. In truth, when a university program cannot afford to hire specialized faculty, it must rely on existing faculty to meet the demands of students asking for educational programs. When a faculty member does not feel comfortable in adopting a specified course that may be considered essential, that course may be dropped and a different course offered that more closely matches the faculty member's teaching interests and expertise.

The fifth reason may be the most critical factor of all: the lack of information for nonprofit management students on alternative problem-solving paradigms. In fact, my concerns about this need were a major factor in my writing this book. On the one hand, I applaud the development and ongoing evolution of the field of non-profit management and the educational and training programs that have facilitated the field's development. On the other hand, I have a concern about the process of where we begin and end our educating and training of individuals as nonprofit managers. Frankly, I do not think we go far enough in our teaching and training (in some cases, we go nowhere at all) regarding alternative decision-making and problem-solving models. Instead, we limit students to the widely accepted and reliable management frameworks and models that have proved to be successful tools. The issue is not with the management models that we do describe and teach about but with the failure to prepare nonprofit managers to handle situations that are unresponsive to these old and reliable management tools.

I believe there is a conservative, and justifiable, predisposition in educational degree and certificate training programs to teach practical and fundamental approaches to managing nonprofit organizations. As one who does both teaching and training, I understand the limitations of time and money that students or institutions of higher education can devote to educational degree and certificate training programs. Given these limitations, our pragmatic approach to educating nonprofit managers boils down to teaching practice methods that seem to work for the majority of situations. In the classroom, we generally focus on formulas and sequential reasoning, such as the following:

"These are steps to creating a budget. First, you . . ."

"These are steps for creating a strategic plan. First, you . . ."

"This is how you run an effective meeting. "First, you . . ."

"This is how you solve problems and disputes. First, you . . ."

We also reinforce the use of gut instinct and commonsense decision making, because most of the time, instinct and common sense work. These straightforward approaches provide the necessary framework to deal with most managerial situations, and so it makes a great deal of sense to convey information that can be easily replicated in the workplace. These clear-cut and uncomplicated approaches can be categorized as "first-order" methodologies for managing a nonprofit organization.

Most of the time, a nonprofit manager's reliance on first-order methods of problem solving and decision making will lead to successful outcomes. My concern is about nonprofit managers who do not have the tools to handle problems that do not respond to first-order approaches. For times when the tools we teach and learn in the classroom do not work, managers need fallback approaches for responding to these problems. Managers who lack this know-how will continue to rely on first-order methods. When first-order approaches fail, the manager typically retraces his or her steps and starts over again, to no avail. In an attempt to find a solution, the manager may repeat this unwinnable cycle over and over, despite the lack of any progress. When ongoing first-order methods are not achieving the intended results, nonprofit managers, board members, and other key stakeholders may experience frustration and conclude that their organization is having chronic and perpetuating problems, which is emblematic of organizational failure.

Because we have not given nonprofit managers assessment and intervention tools that go beyond first-order management approaches, these managers may not recognize when they are contributing to the ongoing nature of the problem. Consequently, they are not capitalizing on the lessons that can be learned from their mistakes.

The Framework and the Steps

It is amazing that so many day-to-day organizational problems are successfully handled through simple processes of problem identification and applying straightforward problem resolution strategies.

But there are exceptions. When routine approaches do not work and problem-solving attempts lead to one unsuccessful effort after another, nonprofit managers can suffer a loss of confidence. In addition, observers can become critical of the managers' abilities. Fortunately, alternative problem resolution approaches are available when routine methods fail.

The alternative approaches presented in this book are based on the idea that there is more than one way to analyze a problem, intervene, and engender change. The objective of this chapter is to introduce the framework and the steps that nonprofit managers can use to design alternative problem resolution strategies.

One of the toughest trials we face in solving difficult problems is changing the way we think about a problem. Our capacity to view problems in alternative ways can be diminished or prejudiced by many factors: our age, cultural orientation, attitudes, personal experience, physical or emotional health, political biases, and numerous other experiences or personality traits that color our view of the world. So being able to resolve unrelenting organizational problems takes a bit of introspection to clarify why we believe the approach that keeps failing us is still the right approach to take. As long as we remain steadfast in a given set of beliefs, management decisions and actions will not vary.

Although it is common to want to stick with a theory or explanation that feels comfortable, effective alternative strategy development requires our acceptance of the idea that our way of thinking about a solution may be flawed. How can this be? Our thinking can be flawed in the same way that we miscalculate our ability to match pieces of a jigsaw puzzle. Only the right combination of puzzle pieces will yield the results that were intended. In trying to put puzzles together, we ordinarily rely on a formula or a commonsense approach that usually works. We select pieces with certain shapes and color combinations that we perceive will match up with other puzzle pieces. Occasionally, we find that pieces that unquestionably look like they should fit together do not. Similarly, managing a difficult problem-solving effort can be a challenge to common sense and sound principles of logic. Sometimes, what you think will work simply does not.

The Basic Framework

The basic framework used in this approach is rooted in some simple scientific methods that we have frequently found to be effective in our personal lives. The steps that we will follow are analogous to the diagnostic procedures employed by physicians. Physicians are taught to diagnose problems by applying various (medically based) theories. These theories serve as a lens through which the physician processes information obtained from interviewing or observing the patient.

Ideally, a physician listens carefully to the patient's description of symptoms or discomfort. At the same time, the physician observes the patient's behaviors and may also ask a myriad of questions as part of fact gathering. Finally, the physician assesses the accumulated information and searches for a medical theory that might explain the patient's complaint and suggest an appropriate treatment.

During this process of diagnosing the patient's problem and devising an appropriate course of treatment, the physician must look at all of the evidence through the lens of his or her medical knowledge. Using this framework, the physician understands that his or her role requires analysis of the facts as they appear through this special lens. Only this type of focus permits the medical practitioner to select a theory of what might be wrong with the patient and then embark on a path to correct the problem.

The physician's assessment of what might be causing the set of symptoms is like formulating a research hypothesis that needs to be tested. The physician uses the formulated hypothesis to select an intervention model that has the best odds of solving the patient's problem. The physician tests this hypothesis about what may be troubling the patient through a medical intervention, such as prescribing medicine or ordering a surgical procedure.

If the intervention does not solve the problem as predicted, the physician's original hypothesis was probably not correct. The next step for the physician would be to factor in the negative results of the first intervention and use the negative results as additional data. After synthesizing the new data with the preexisting information, the physician searches his or her knowledge base for a different theory that might help explain what is wrong with the patient. This process of medical inquiry, theory building, and intervention would be repeated until the patient's problems have been resolved.

Nonprofit managers can learn to critically examine an organizational issue using many of the same steps that the physician uses in the diagnostic process and the development of intervention strategies. Managers can, for example, gather data about the duration of the organizational problem, such as its intensity and its effects on others, and what types of interventions were tried that failed.

After establishing a pool of substantive information, the manager would draw on his or her knowledge of various organizational behavior theories or turn to some supporting literature to identify a theory that can be generalized to the problem. The nonprofit manager would select a theory that can aid comprehension of the issues and help in assessing the breadth and depth of the organization's problems. Sometimes it is necessary to use more than one theory to view a problem. By exploring the problem with more than one theory, we increase the number of perspectives from which we view the problem. That multitheory approach may expand our thinking, lead us to multiple thoughts about the problem, and help us devise alternative problem resolutions and planned change strategies. Having diagnosed the problem in this way, the nonprofit manager can then design an organizational development strategy for resolving problems and achieving organizational success.

Theory-based models can help us view problems in unique ways that might otherwise go unnoticed. Using different theories to examine organizational issues is like using a lens of a different color or a different strength to view an object. In using a different lens to view the sky and clouds, for example, the sky and clouds would not have changed, but our perception of them would be different. This perceptual difference allows us to think about the sky and clouds in a multidimensional way. Similarly, if we use the lens as a filter to alter our perception of an organizational issue, we may see it in a new dimension even though the original situation would not have changed. By examining an issue through different eyes, we can formulate alternative solutions to it.

Where do the theories that will help us resolve nonprofit management problems come from? Theories can be borrowed from the management sciences, psychology, sociology, and other applied fields. Nonprofit managers can either study and memorize a number of theories—as the physician memorizes a number of medical theories—or, when a theory is needed, they can simply review the literature that describes organizational theories and search for the one that fits the particular set of circumstances. Some of the theories that are used in our case studies are briefly described in the Appendix.

In summary, the steps that the nonprofit manager will follow for assessing problems that do not seem to react to the usual straightforward problem-solving methods are these:

1. Gather the facts about the problem that could not be resolved through the standard (first-order) approach.

2. Disclose the beliefs that guided the intervention that did not work in this situation.

3. Select one or more theories to use as a lens to examine the issues.

4. Come up with a hypothesis that will guide planned change.

5. Devise an alternative intervention strategy based on the hypothesis (this is known as taking a second-order approach).

6. Implement the new strategy.

7. Evaluate the results.

8. If the problem remains unresolved, repeat the steps.

4

First-Order and Second-Order Approaches to Change

Having stated in Chapter Three that there are several organizational theories that we can use to help us understand nonprofit organizational behavior, I need now to clarify that the concepts of "first-order" and "second-order" approaches to problems and solutions are exempt from that claim. These two concepts are fundamental to the success of the alternative approach exemplified in this book. The purpose of this chapter is to equip nonprofit managers with the means to classify first-order and second-order approaches to problem resolution and planned change in any nonprofit organization.

Some nonprofit managers who are unfamiliar with this approach may have experienced success by instinctually moving from first-order to second-order change. Because nonprofit organizational success is much too important to leave to instinct alone, it is imperative that nonprofit managers have the ability to consciously differentiate between these two concepts. Nonprofit managers who have developed this capacity will have a greater facility for resolving thorny problems and promoting organizational change.

This chapter is intended to provide nonprofit managers with the basic foundation for building intervention strategies that work; it is a primer on first-order and second-order approaches. A personal experience may be illustrative. In my initial attempt at writing this chapter, I found that as I tried to put in plain words how these two concepts work, my results became obscured, the task became more complicated, and the purpose of the chapter went off course. In my attempt to resolve this writing dilemma, I discovered that my experience modeled a first-order and second-order problem resolution approach. In other words, the more that I tried writing the chapter in one style to avoid using a social science type of taxonomy, the more problematic it became to write the chapter. As long as I kept thinking the same way about how I must write this chapter, the more I failed at the task. Over and over it became a frustrating experience. This was an example of persisting with a first-order solution that did not work. As long as I stayed within the parameters of an idealized (first-order) approach, I was unable to make progress. When I abandoned the artificial constraints that had boxed me in to looking at only a first-order method, I was able to step out of the problem, change my approach, and produce a chapter that is a hybrid between a classroom lecture and a conversation.

Organizational change can happen in a haphazard way, or it can be planned. Whether by intention or by chance, the process of change can lead to beneficial outcomes or can turn out badly for the organization and its employees, volunteers, and clients. To improve the likelihood that change will be for the better, it is always best for the executive director and his or her managers to be in control of a change effort. Being in control and thus introducing organizational change in a purposeful way is known as a planned change effort. We use planned change in two ways. It is used to accomplish new initiatives or it is used as a tool to correct and resolve problematic situations.

Planned change can occur by either of two managerial methods, known as first-order and second-order approaches. Change attempts using first-order means do not require a shift in the customary way of thinking about a problem or its intended solution. By contrast, second-order change requires a shift in how one interprets a problem and implements a series of activities aimed at solving problems and achieving organizational change.

In the late 1960s and early 1970s, researchers at the Mental Research Institute in Palo Alto, California, examined the concepts of change and problem resolution (see Watzlawick, Weakland, Fisch, and Erickson, 1974). Although they were professionally interested in change and human behavior in the context of applied psychotherapy, their principles regarding why people change or do not change have uncanny relevance for understanding how problems arise and are subsequently resolved or perpetuated in nonprofit organizations.

Specifically, the researchers in Palo Alto observed that some problems did not improve following interventions that were intended to improve them. These researchers came to believe through research observation that if an intended solution does not alter the structure of the problem, the existing problem will remain the same or worsen. They referred to these failed attempts as occurring in the "first order," often relying on "more of the same" or repetitive solutions and simply missing the need for a more radical style of intervention.

Our everyday common approach to solving problems involves first-order change, but we typically don't use this terminology in the workplace. Our use of first-order change methods generally works to resolve problems and does not require sweeping or comprehensive reorganization.

When second-order methods are used, they generally lead to noticeable organizational transformations. Second-order change techniques often focus on altering the target of the first-order change attempt that did not work. In other words, what was thought to be the solution in the first-order change effort would actually become one of the key targets of the second-order intervention. Someone once said that the seed of the solution is always present in the problem; its advantages are just misunderstood.

Researchers typically suggest that the focus of management change efforts should be on the "what," that is, *What is happening in the here and now that is perpetuating the problem?* It is important not to get stuck on the "why" of a problem. Focusing on the "why " is a first-order approach and a natural starting place for most individuals, according to these Palo Alto researchers. When enlightenment does not clear a path for transforming organizational problems, a new method of intervention should be sought. An ongoing attempt to seek insight using a first-order method of intervention will just frustrate continuing change efforts.

The researchers use their own scholarly formulation to explain how problem-solving approaches can actually perpetuate failure (Watzlawick, Weakland, Fisch, and Erickson, 1974, p. 90): "An event (a) is about to take place, but (a) is undesirable. Common sense suggests its prevention or avoidance is by means of the reciprocal or opposite, that is, (not-a). As long as the solution is sought within this dichotomy of (a) and (not-a)," the problem will be perpetuated because the structure of the problem has not been altered. This dilemma is an example of first-order change. Attempted solutions of the first order will sometimes be the same as applying commonsense logic. Whatever the first-order strategy is, it will not lead to extensive organizational change.

When the first-order solution does not work, there is an inclination to repeat the same solution over and over. Another way of explaining this repetitive problem-solving attempt is that individuals approach an issue in the only way they know how. If a person does not know to act differently, they generally do more of the same, more of what they know. Instead of detaching themselves from the thought processes that proved ineffective in solving the problem, they hamper progress by relying on the same old solution. In this way, the intended solution only intensifies the problem and exacerbates the overall sense of management and organizational failure. Because the intended (first-order) solution becomes part of the problem, second-order change efforts may need to target the first-order approach that fueled the problem.

Peter Brill and Richard Worth (1997, pp. 29–30) liken the first-order change process to the face on a clock: "The hands move around a fixed set of numbers, but nothing ever really changes." They further explain, "Systems often tend to reach equilibrium with self-reinforcing cycles that keep fundamental change from occurring." However, it is important to recognize that second-order change should not automatically supplant the use of first-order attempts. First-order change, in fact, is very important to the smooth operation of a nonprofit organization. For example, if an opening on a board of directors exists, filling the board position with a new member may constitute a change to the board composition, but it does not cause a radical change. Here the first-order change process of adding a board member is intended for the purpose of maintaining stability, and in large part the board culture remains the same.

First-order change processes work for some problems, but when a more fundamental change must occur, a more far-reaching approach must be used. To achieve an essential change beyond the first-order type, the problem solver must change his or her lens in order to view the construct of the problem differently. By examining the construct of the problem in a different light, the problem solver can see more than one way to approach problem resolution and effect change. To break the cycle that kept the problem intact, a second-order type of change is necessary. The formula for second-order change is "(not-a) but also not (not-a)." It's a solution that often contradicts common sense. To apply this formula effectively, the problem solver must change his or her rules about problem solving. The behavior that is needed can be characterized by the expression "thinking out of the box."

By thinking out of the box, effective problem solvers change the way they view and interpret problems. Innovative thinkers may understand that the "why" of a problem might be intellectually interesting, but they also know that they do not always need to comprehend the "why" of the problem or understand a problem's origin or how it evolved. Instead, effective problem solvers can initiate change by focusing on the present effects of the problem. Consider the age-old concern of a board member who misses several board meetings. An intervention of the first-order change type might have the executive director or board chair inform the board member about the importance of attending meetings. The board member might be reminded of the attendance requirements outlined in the bylaws or in a general job description for board members. Or the board member might be provided with reading materials that outline the duties of board members. We already know from experience in the field that explaining this important facet of a board member's responsibility does not lead to long-term changes in attendance behavior.

Understanding the reason why a board member could not attend meetings on a regular basis does not help alter the attendance issue or make other board members feel better about their colleague's absence. The "why" merely provides information that can be shared with the board members who are present, such as, "Fred cannot be here this evening because he has a dental appointment!" Knowing that the board member went to the dentist really does not help us understand the underlying motivation for the frequent absences. It is a safe bet that this board member's attendance at board meetings will continue to be spotty if the problem solver repeatedly uses the first-order approach.

A successful change effort must foresee a change in the structural issues (*a* and *not-a*) that underpin the problem. The solution may require a realignment of board responsibilities, such as making staff responsible for a board member's participation, or establish different modes of board participation, such as involvement by telephone. For example, Fred could have gone to the dentist but still participate in the board meeting using a headphone or a wireless telephone. Even if Fred could not talk during the dental procedures, he could listen to the discussion and could vote by signaling his decision by pressing on the telephone keys that emit a tone: one key tone for a yes vote, two for a no vote, and three for an abstention.

By allowing for this type of second-order change, the problem of not being physically present in the same room with other board members becomes a moot issue. Given the relatively inexpensive communication technology that is available, a board member's physical presence is no longer essential to participation. Also, instead of being dependent on whether the board member makes an appearance in the boardroom, a staff member can take the initiative of calling or paging the board member to ensure that the board member is connected to the meeting. In this way, the "more of the same" approach of reminding the board member about roles and responsibilities can be shelved. The responsibility for participation in board meetings does not have to be the burden of the board member alone; it can be creatively shared among the board member and staff.

When a "more of the same" approach does not lead to essential and long-term changes, such as board participation in our example, a second-order tool can be used to provide a different perception of the problem. The technique is known as reframing. Reframing is intended to alter one's perception of an event. Consider the example of trying to redecorate one's home to project a different image. One may have one's sofa reupholstered or use a different style of matting and framing materials around one's artwork. In both of these situations, the structure of the sofa and the original nature of the artwork did not change, yet a new cover, new matting, and a new frame immediately alter the way those items look. The change of appearance leads to different ways of looking at objects. The art of reframing works the same way. By giving an event a different meaning, we alter the way the event is perceived, triggering different reactions to the event.

Taking the board attendance issue as an example, we can see how the second-order change technique of reframing works. Instead of categorizing this board member's lack of attendance a problem, we can reframe nonattendance so that it is not considered a major problem. We explain the nonattendance in the following way:

- Because our board members are important and busy people, it would not be reasonable to expect that they would be available to participate in all of the board meetings.

- Because our board members have many obligations, we must make use of available communication technology if we want their participation.

- Because our board members must balance their work, family, and board responsibilities, the staff can help relieve some of the pressure by helping board members fulfill their responsibilities.

In these three bulleted statements, we have redefined a situation in a way that gives the issue of attendance a different emphasis. Through creative interpretation, we gave the events new meaning. The issue of nonattendance at board meetings went from being a common governance problem and an annoyance to being viewed as a reasonable expectation of trying to involve busy board members. We have literally reframed the situation so that our perception of the board member's behavior is altered. This allows us to see the board member in a new light. The intervention targeted the viewpoint that the board member's spotty meeting attendance was a sign of irresponsible and noncommittal behavior. Through reframing, a cognitive shift occurred, and we now interpret the board member's spotty attendance as a reflection of the fact that very busy and important individuals serve on the organization's governing board. Having a board comprised of busy and important individuals may increase an organization's visibility and credibility. It is certainly far more palatable to be associated with important individuals than burdened with irresponsible board members!

In our use of a second-order framework in this example, we adopted the view that to achieve active and successful board members, there may need to be a shared responsibility among the board member and a staff member whose role is to find ways to make the board members' effective participation a reality. This expansion of a staff role to assisting board members—who are ordinarily expected to be active and effective in their own right—may not be an acceptable approach for nonprofit managers who have a traditionalist orientation toward nonprofit governance or a traditionalist view of organizational behavior. For second-order interventions to be applied effectively, nonprofit managers need to be flexible and willing to expand their zone of comfort by trying the extraordinary. Sometimes this means breaking old traditions and writing new rules.

To learn how to think differently and know when second-order change tools should be used, initially observe people using your standard first-order approach. If the outcome was not what you wanted, observe how often the first-order change effort is repeated unproductively. When efforts produce more-of-the-same results, that should be a signal to intervene with second-order methods.

Why would someone continue to repeat a first-order approach if it continually leads to failure? Problem solvers are usually not aware of what they are doing to cause a problem to perpetuate. For example, consider an individual who was seeking a solution by brainstorming ideas, either in a group or in a self-directed exercise. It would be common for an individual to try solving the organizational problem by using one of the reasonable-sounding suggestions that surfaced during the brainstorming exercise. Characteristically, the ranges of options that an individual is drawn to are those that he or she has tried in the past. There is a tendency to gravitate toward the familiar and persist at trying an intended solution even if it did not work in the past.

Three factors contribute to making decisions that get stuck at the first-order level. One is a lack of experience as a decision maker. Regardless of a person's level of intellect, the ability to examine a problem analytically generally improves with years of experience. While it is also true that years of experience can lead to many years of practicing bad habits in one's approach to problem solving, experience often increases a person's ability to differentiate more serious problems from less serious ones.

A second factor is whether the problem solver can engage in abstract reasoning. For example, once an art critic commented to Cézanne that his impressionistic painting "doesn't look anything like a sunset." Upon examining the painting, Cézanne replied,

"Then you don't see sunsets like I do" (Bolman and Deal, 1997, p. 12). The point is that some people are more concrete in their thinking. Without the ability to think abstractly, an individual may have difficulty seeing multiple messages that are produced in words and behaviors, such as differentiating meaning through tone, choice of wording, and body language.

A third contributing factor to persistent attempts at first-order change may be the personal difficulty that individuals have in separating their emotions from the problem that needs to be solved. Sometimes an individual can be "tied in" to a problem because of personal experiences. In these circumstances, the problem solver can make rash decisions in an attempt to avoid dealing with the issues or may simply lack the objectivity to analyze the situation and take the appropriate steps necessary to resolve the problem.

Devising problem-solving efforts to achieve a fundamental second-order change is not an easy assignment. Machiavelli observed, "It must be realized that there is nothing more difficult to plan, more uncertain of success, or more dangerous to manage than the establishment of a new order of [things]" (Bolman and Deal, 1997, p. 320). To bring about a second-order type of change, the problem solver should have some fundamental management ability to control his or her environment. Like a successful chess player, the manager who takes the time to map out the trail of a decision is likely to make better game decisions than the player who is too eager and takes action before realizing that certain moves will be more costly in the long run.

The type of understanding we want to achieve requires the problem solver to perceive the component parts of the problem and focus on their interrelationships. We are not very interested in the root of the problem, asking questions that would help us understand why the problem exists. In our chess example, the decision maker needs to know how each chess piece moves, its value in the game, and some probabilities about alternative decisions that the opponent might make in response to one's own game decisions. These things are more important than knowing why each piece is allowed to move only in the manner that the rules allow.

Just as some people are better chess players than others, some people are more skilled and more knowledgeable about the process of diagnosing nonprofit problems and designing organizational change efforts. In my opinion, the effective nonprofit executive director and other nonprofit managers must be able to distinguish when to use a first-order change and when a second-order change is warranted. It would be helpful, too, if board members, to support management staff intervention efforts, also understood the conceptual differences between first-order and second-order change, but I do not advocate a board member's involvement in management-level decisions.

The capability to distinguish between intervening with either first-order or second-order methods will improve with practice and by staying focused on the dynamics of the problems and avoiding the trap of seeking out the etiology of the problem. Furthermore, it is important that managers not jump to a quick diagnosis and impulsively implement a plan for intervention. Instead, it is more important that the manager take the time to look for patterns of behavior that seem to promote rather than resolve problematic organizational issues.

Although problem resolution efforts require an identification of the issues, nonprofit managers who have the facility to differentiate between first-order and second-order change may find themselves in disagreements with other managers who are unfamiliar with the first- and second-order concepts. Operating alongside someone without this knowledge can be frustrating for both managers. In such situations, it is generally best not to engage in a debate over theoretical frameworks but rather to decide who will be in charge of the problem resolution and intervention efforts.

The nonprofit manager who has the capacity to examine problems by using alternative frameworks should try to view the situation in the way that the colleague sees the world, but only as a tool to broaden understanding of the colleague's perspective. This sensitivity may help in trying to explain the choice of intervention using the style of language that is best understood by the other manager.

In summary, the nonprofit manager needs to determine whether the change effort should be of the first-order or second-order type. If many solutions have been tried and change efforts have done little to resolve organizational issues, it is likely that a more radical and more fundamental approach of the second-order kind might be required.

Part II

Seven Tough Problems
and How to Solve Them

The seven chapters in Part II highlight through case studies some tough and recognizable problems that we often see in nonprofit organizations. Each chapter lays out the problem, which is then followed by a case study. Using various organizational behavior theories, each chapter provides an analysis of the case study and demonstrates how potential solutions are derived and implemented. Finally, each chapter reports the results of the implementation of alternative problem resolution and change strategies.

Resource A at the back of the book describes several of the theories that are used to tackle the seven tough problems. Referring to Resource A can be a useful way to further your understanding of why certain theories were selected for analyzing the problems and suggesting potential solutions.

5

Recruitment Disorientation

The Problem

Countless numbers of individuals have been recruited to serve as volunteer board members without ever being informed of their role or the organization's expectations of them. Consequently, those board members may not be fulfilling their essential duties—not out of disregard for their board member position but because they are simply uninformed.

Naturally, a board member who is unaware of performance expectations that are held by other board members or by the executive director of the nonprofit organization may unwittingly appear to be irresponsible for failing to fulfill certain (unspoken) obligations.

This is no small problem. In written and verbal surveys that I have conducted, many hundreds of board members all over the United States reported accepting invitations to become board members without any understanding of the level of commitment they were making. Many reported that if they had been fully informed of the scope of board members' duties, they would have declined the invitation at the start.

Seeing that each nonprofit organization may have different expectations of its board members or emphasize certain governance activities over others, it would be both respectful and ethical to educate prospective board members of the full range of activities that they may be required to perform. Also, it is unfair to assume that individuals who have previously served on a nonprofit board would automatically know what is expected of them by another nonprofit organization. There may be overlap, but the differences may be enough to make it impossible for a board member to perform at a quality level or dissuade the person from putting the requisite energy into the new board role.

By not providing board prospects with well-defined expectations, it is difficult and unfair to hold them accountable for their limited involvement. Several types of problems can occur when role-clarifying information is not shared with board candidates during the recruitment phase. Because pervasive problems result from inadequate orientation, the term "recruitment disorientation" is fitting.

Individuals who are disoriented regarding their role as board member are more likely to exhibit a range of behaviors that are generally considered problematic. These behaviors include irregular attendance at board meetings, frequently leaving board meetings early, coming to meetings late, not participating in organizational events, failing to meet fundraising obligations, declining committee assignments, and making little or no personal financial contribution to the organization.

This cluster of symptoms depicts the board member as being apathetic, disloyal, unresponsive, and uncaring. Deleterious labels such as these get pinned to individual board members as though the problematic behaviors stem from the individual board member's persona instead of recognizing the behaviors as the unintended consequences that result from ineffective methods of board member recruitment.

Unfortunately, the link between board member behaviors that are perceived as impassive and ineffectual and the organization's unproductive recruitment methods becomes blurred. In other words, the presenting problem as usually stated by the nonprofit manager (and sometimes by other board members) is that "we have board members who lack commitment and do not follow through with their board responsibilities. What can we do to get rid of them," they ask, "or to make them more responsible and committed?"

The Case Study

The common symptomatic conditions of inattentiveness and mediocre board performance are spotlighted in the following case study of recruitment disorientation that occurred in a medium-sized nonprofit organization in Centennial, Colorado. KidsCan, Inc., provides counseling and tutorial services for adolescent boys and girls with mild to moderate emotional and learning problems.

Similar to many executive directors and board members of nonprofit organizations, Greg McKay, the executive director of Kids-Can, Inc., was not aware of the underlying condition of recruitment disorientation, its dynamics, or how he and his board members may have contributed to certain board performance issues.

Like most nonprofit organizations, KidsCan expected its board members to help solve problems, represent the organization in the community, develop and use important contacts, serve on committees, and help raise money. Notwithstanding some difficulties in seeing these expectations fulfilled, Greg was concerned about a "faction" of board members who had spotty attendance at board meetings, did not stay for entire meetings, did not accept committee assignments, did not make financial contributions, and did not attend special events. Greg reported four attempts that he had made to rectify board member commitment and performance concerns.

Attempt 1

Based on his reading and workshops he attended, Greg believed that the root of the problem was that board members did not really know each other. He reasoned that if the relationships among board members were enhanced, they would feel a stronger commitment to each other, leading to greater board member participation and follow-through. To achieve this end, Greg focused on the development and implementation of a board retreat that would encourage board member interaction. What happened was that some board members did not show and some left early.

Attempt 2

In his second attempt, Greg opted to try a couple of the good tips that were shared at one of the workshops he attended at the statewide membership association of nonprofit organizations' annual conference, "Improving the Nonprofit Organization: Achieving Collaboration Through Leadership and Example." Specifically, Greg tried to improve board member attendance by increasing the different ways the board would be notified of board meetings. The idea was based on a marketing strategy about getting the (product) name out so many times before people really pay attention to the message.

Two weeks before the meeting, a written notice and packet of materials were sent by mail. Three days later, Greg e-mailed the board members with a reminder. Around the same time, Greg's executive assistant called each board member by phone to ask if he or she had received the mailed packet. If the board member could not be reached directly, a message was left with an assistant or as voice mail. The message included a reminder of the meeting day, date, and time.

Attendance did not improve with these extra notices.

Attempt 3

Greg received a promotional brochure in the mail reporting favorable outcomes for organizations all over the United States and Canada who used a set of commercially produced board-training videos with accompanying workbooks. Greg invested in the video and workbook package, convinced by the brochure's testimonial from a board chair: "I could not believe the improvement in the board's attendance and participation. I was so encouraged that I took out my checkbook and agreed to serve another term."

After reviewing the tapes and workbooks with Dr. Anne Miller, the KidsCan board chair, the two decided that they would show one segment of the videotape at the start of every board meeting and then encourage a fifteen-minute discussion among board members using the outline from the workbooks.

What occurred was that two board members left the room while the tape was playing in order to make cellular phone calls. Following the playing of the tape, very limited dialogue occurred among the board members.

Attempt 4

Greg read in the workbook and heard on one of the videotapes that the board chair's role was more important than just facilitating board meetings. The message described the board chair as "being in charge" and needing to demonstrate that "leadership starts at the top." Greg believed that if Anne took her role more seriously, the other board members would follow suit.

What occurred after the board chair reviewed the videotape was a recognition that she could not live up to the expectations that were presented. Anne resigned.

Analysis of the Case

When Greg first approached me to discuss his organizational concerns, his entire presentation focused on a presenting problem that consisted of a number of disconcerting board member behaviors. Greg described his frustration and his lack of success in four attempts to address the issues of board member commitment, attendance, and performance. As with many presenting problems, the focus of Greg's concern was actually the symptoms of the primary problem.

Executive directors and board members typically overlook the relationship between lackluster board performance and the organization's recruitment procedures. It is understandable that these events may not appear to be associated with each other since they occur sequentially and not simultaneously. For that matter, to most observers, the symptomatic problems of ineffective board participation that emerge from recruitment disorientation also appear to be quite independent of each other. As a result of the lag time between the cause and its effects, board recruitment is viewed as a distinct activity that is not commonly linked to later board member performance.

As a result of his limited success, it is understandable that Greg would feel frustrated and defeated. It appears that all of Greg's assessments and interventions were of the first-order type. Each was a straightforward and reasonable attempt at rectification in reaction to Greg's assessment and his beliefs that the presenting problem was indeed the problem. Had Greg viewed the presenting problem using a different lens or theoretical framework, he probably would have altered his responses long before he ever reached his fourth attempt at change. By using the same paradigm for each of his interventions, Greg continued to miss the targets for change. Consequently, he continued on the path of frustration and failure. Let us briefly examine each of his four attempts.

Analysis of Attempt 1

What was wrong with Greg's first attempted solution? There was nothing wrong with the idea of a board retreat. The retreat might have been more productive if the board had perceived the original need for one and established an agenda to meet certain objectives, but since the board did not recognize the need, coaxing the idea along seemed like a reasonable executive director effort. Greg thought that if he could get the board members in a social setting, they would build trust and a bond that would translate into more effective board member participation. That seemed like a reasonable hypothesis. However, in this situation, it was not the correct hypothesis for resolving his concerns about board member participation.

Because the patterns of individual board member behaviors took root during the recruitment stage, the undoing of this problem would not be solved by having board members attend a retreat. In fact, with some absenteeism and some board members leaving for home before the retreat adjourned, the retreat was simply a microcosm of all the typical board member issues that Greg had wanted to curb.

Analysis of Attempt 2

In his second attempt, Greg applied one of the "best practices" of meeting management. He sent regular meeting reminders using different formats of communication. There were no flaws in using various approaches for reminding board members about their upcoming meetings. In this case, the gain was negligible because the problems of board attendance and participation were unrelated to having knowledge of when meetings were being held. In fact, it was widely known that meetings were held on the third Thursday of the month. Therefore, the intended solution did not work because Greg's hypothesis missed the target of the problem. His problem-solving effort was an example of the first-order, "more of the same" type.

Analysis of Attempt 3

One cannot argue strongly against the value of board development training. It can be a sound practice for educating board members about their roles and responsibilities. Therefore, it was understandable why Greg would get his hopes up after reading favorable endorsements for the videotapes and workbooks that he eventually purchased. Why didn't the tapes produce the type of outcome that Greg was seeking?

Let's start with the most obvious: it is very likely that this board, like so many others, were already familiar with the board dos and don'ts that comprised the key message in each of the video lessons. As a first-order intervention, providing an indirect form of a lecture on board responsibilities generally is not a successful approach for motivating board member participation.

Analysis of Attempt 4

Greg's fourth attempt backfired. Greg's board chair was perfectly content in her role until Greg had her view the videotape that conveyed the message that she was not doing an effective job and needed to change her leadership style. Pointing out the board chair's weakness as a leader only helped Anne bring into focus that she would not be able to do the job in the way that Greg would prefer. His attempted solution placed Anne in an untenable position. If she continued as board chair, she would know that she was not performing at the level that was expected of her. Furthermore, if Greg and others discouraged her act of resignation, they were communicating a message of acceptance for mediocrity and the status quo.

In this case, Anne's solution was to quit. Her reaction makes perfect sense, as it was the only way out of the dilemma. Paradoxically, after recognizing that she could not fulfill the leadership tasks that were required of her, Anne's resignation turned out to be the ultimate act of a leader who understands that stepping down would be in the best interest of the organization.

The Solution

Before an intervention strategy can be developed, there are important preparatory stages.

If there were only one isolated case of a board member not performing his or her duties, it would not lead to a "diagnosis" of recruitment disorientation. Generally, if recruitment disorientation exists, the symptoms would be demonstrated through the behaviors of more than one board member. The "presenting problems" that stem from recruitment disorientation are powerful restraining forces. They include the following:

- Inconsistent commitments to tasks

- Spotty attendance at board or committee meetings

- Limited or no follow-through on assignments

- Limited or no involvement in organizational events

- Avoidance of fundraising and making no financial contribution to the organization

Because the symptoms of recruitment disorientation blossom long after the problem has been planted, the major goal needs to be to avoid recruitment disorientation through prevention and best practices. The elimination of recruitment disorientation is essential for achieving governance success.

First-Order or Second-Order Approach?

Not only did all four of Greg's problem-solving efforts fail, but each attempted solution only reinforced how Greg felt about the problems and made him even more fixated on solving his problem with his board.

Greg did not link his concerns about board member involvement to board recruitment efforts. He viewed the limitations of board member participation as the end result, and the cause of those behaviors was thought to be the lack of board member caring and commitment. Greg's interventions led to some unintended and unfortunate consequences—worst of all, the resignation of the board chair. This outcome illustrates how a problem can perpetuate and escalate when an intended solution does not address the real underlying cause of the difficulties.

When simple first-order change attempts do not produce the type of outcome that was anticipated, a second-order change approach should be considered. The use of second-order change techniques is intended to move the situation away from the traps left untouched by the application of first-order problem-solving efforts.

Selecting Theories for Examining the Issues

One way of looking at the problem of recruitment disorientation is through the lens of the Lewin Force Field Analysis approach. By applying this theory, the objective becomes one of detecting the forces that are restraining the type of change that we are attempting to achieve. Accordingly, Greg was unable to invoke organizational behavior change because he did not differentiate between driving forces and restraining forces.

In this case, the planned approach would be to systematically and consistently apply driving forces during the recruiting and candidacy identification stages. At these early cultivation stages—before an individual is asked to make a commitment to become a board member—it would be proper to communicate the rules about board member participation. Prospects should be informed about expectations of board attendance, committee involvement, personal contributions, and fundraising.

I have found that the most effective approach to recruitment and cultivation of board prospects is when the process is viewed as a year-round activity, including periods of time when there are no immediate vacancies. The search for an ideal board candidate who has specific skills or knowledge is a time-consuming and arduous process. Consequently, volunteers may not be able to devote the requisite number of hours that it may take to identify appropriate board candidates. By attempting to short-circuit recruiting and nomination procedures, some important developmental activities that should be intrinsic to developing relationships with potential board prospects are sacrificed. Using the quickest and easiest way to select board candidates portends trouble and lays the foundation for recruitment disorientation to become entrenched.

Formulating a Hypothesis to Guide Planned Change

As part of our mutual attempt to solve his organizational difficulties, I asked Greg to examine the issues of board involvement from the point of view of a communication model. Hypothetically, the symptoms or presenting problems could be seen as symbolic and representative behaviors and not the actual problem.

By overlaying a communication model, Greg would be able to avoid interpreting the symptomatic behaviors as those of uncaring and uncommitted board behavior and instead view these symptoms as signaling behaviors.

Devising an Alternative Intervention Strategy Based on the Hypothesis

I saw Greg's organizational problems as having two major components. In one part, the causes of recruitment disorientation needed to be addressed to prevent similar problems from surfacing in the future. The second part required attention to the current reality. This included responding to Greg's frustration, which may have been getting in the way of his being as effective as possible. Also, some effort would be necessary to improve board participation, especially attendance of board members who stay for only a portion of a board meeting. Board member participation could not be overlooked because these board members might remain on the board for years, given the right to serve two consecutive three-year terms under the board's rotation policy.

The approach that I took for the second part of the problem also had two steps to it. The first step was to assist Greg in reframing his outlook about the conceptual standards of board participation. Although Greg's state of frustration was understandable, in my view, Greg also had unrealistic expectations of his board members. I challenged Greg to confront his own belief system about governing boards by asking, "Why are you holding your board members to ideal standards of participation when they have demonstrated that these standards are too difficult for them to achieve?"

Instead of being frustrated and angry by holding on to certain rigid beliefs about what a board should be doing, I thought, it might make more sense for Greg to resolve his issues by altering (reframing) his own expectations about board member involvement. In other words, if Greg eliminated or revised his standards to a more reasonable set of objectives that would fit the composition of his current board, he would feel more satisfied with his board's performance. Very simply, if Greg could change his expectations and not expect a textbook set of behaviors from his board of directors, accepting a lesser level of involvement and leadership from these individuals, he would not become as disturbed when they did not perform at such an idealized level.

As a reframing tool, this change in personal expectations with respect to these board members incorporated the limitations of what these individuals could reasonably do as volunteers, especially in light of their obligations to their families and careers.

Does this mean Greg should simply look the other way and not expect board member involvement? Not at all! The idea is to attain a level of board involvement that is practical and achievable in light of the fact that many of Greg's board members did not know what they were getting into by accepting their invitation to serve on the KidsCan board. The board should be held to some reasonable level of expectations.

The second step is a more complex example of a second-order change technique. This application was to address the chronic issue of board members leaving board meetings early but staying long enough to be recorded as present. This issue could not be ignored because it undermined the board's ability to conduct a reasonable dialogue and exchange of opinion prior to making policy decisions.

On several occasions, the number of board members would dwindle below quorum level, and official action could not be taken. This was an upsetting situation for the board members who would diligently honor the start and end times for their board meetings.

Implementing the New Strategy

To initiate the second-order change effort, I met with Greg and his new board chair, Sam Engles. After discussing the attendance issue, I told them that I had a plan that I thought would reasonably improve attendance. Because second-order interventions are not as straightforward as first-order approaches, the second-order plan might sound strange to someone who does not think in those terms. I asked them to make a commitment to following through even if they thought the plan struck them as odd or unusual. They were further requested not to reveal the plan to the other board members, other than to say that they had met with me and that they were following through on my recommendations on how to improve the effectiveness of the board's operations.

Greg and Sam agreed to carry out my instructions. I told them that I believed that not only would their actions demonstrate their flexibility as leaders, but they would also prevent the onset of frustration and anger often experienced by the board members left behind by colleagues getting up and leaving when crucial matters remained to be discussed.

At the beginning of the next board meeting, Sam asked all the board members to write on a 3-by-5-inch card what time they planned to leave the meeting. They were also asked not to write their name on the card. After Greg collected and examined the cards, he gave Sam the card that had the earliest departure time written on it. About ten minutes before this earliest departure time, Sam announced that "due to the importance of having everyone participate and to ensure that we all hear the same information—because it is so difficult to put into the minutes the fine details and rich subtleties of discussion—we shall adjourn the meeting in about ten minutes to accommodate our fellow board members who indicated their need to leave earlier than we had originally planned."

The procedural directions that I gave to Sam and Greg were designed to ensure adjournment of their board meeting before any board members walked out. The intent was to reframe and gain control over the disruption caused by the usual early departure. Since early departures would ordinarily undercut this board's ability to conduct its business effectively, having the entire group leave early did not prevent the board from completing its business. The idea of the reframe was to conceptualize the board as one entity and not as a collection of ten individuals who could come and go as they pleased.

Sam had been instructed to follow this procedure and repeat the same script at the start of the next board meeting. By the third board meeting following the first reframing intervention, the board members' departure times were closer to the intended evening's agenda and time limits! By the fifth board meeting, some new organizational behaviors also were evident. Board members were writing down their intentions to stay until the end of the meeting. Another new event occurred: two board members actually telephoned to say that they were not going to attend the meeting (instead of coming to the meeting and leaving within thirty minutes, thereby forcing the entire meeting to end prematurely). Because of the nature of the original recruitment disorientation problem, our solution required an all-or-nothing approach. It would not have worked to tell these two board members to come and leave when they needed to leave. That would have set the group back on its early course of not honoring a time commitment and their work.

In this example, the executive director and board chair achieved a second-order change by taking control of the early departure problem. Instead of board members getting frustrated with those who would leave early, the adjournment time was now controlled by the board chair. Sam reframed the disruption of exiting behavior. His requirement that everyone leave early symbolically demonstrated the importance of the board's operating as a collective.

Through rule-changing actions, the executive director and board chair displaced the conceptual and emotional viewpoint about board members leaving early. In fact, they changed the entire meaning of early departure. The fact that some board members chose not to attend a meeting instead of attending for part of the meeting and then leaving early was then reframed to be viewed as a reasonable decision. Attending for only a short period of time and then causing a disruption of the entire meeting is a different class of problem, one that is less acceptable than calling to announce that one will not be able to participate in the meeting.

Second-order change strategies have to be tailored to the group and its unique situation. Whatever message is developed for this purpose, it is ethically important that the facts and content of the message fit the situation. In this case, I asked Sam to read the script when it was time for him to state his message to the board about adjourning the meeting. Having Sam read the message and not speak extemporaneously ensured that the content would be conveyed as intended and consistently from meeting to meeting. In addition, Sam's reading would ensure that his intonation would be measured and controlled, making it less likely that he would communicate a subliminal message that could subvert the exercise. (For example, it is possible through tone of voice and body language to convey a message that could be interpreted as "We're ending the meeting before Harry has the chance to ruin everything as he usually does by leaving early and before everyone gets upset and angry." If a subliminal message of that type were transmitted, it would alter the intervention to a first-order type exercise, and probably little would change.)

Additional Considerations

Clarifying and communicating board role expectations sounds like a simplistic solution, but in reality, its application is complex and time-consuming, albeit within the boundaries of a first-order approach.

It takes a great deal more time to methodically select board prospects and inform nominees about the organization's mission and vision than simply to extend invitations to serve. When recruiting is haphazard, boards cannot really be sure that they are attracting responsible decision makers who will act prudently and not run afoul of the board's legal and ethical responsibilities.

To prevent recruitment disorientation, the nonprofit should approach the board recruitment task in much the same way that a "headhunter" searches for a perfect job candidate:

- Do not wait for the perfect board candidate to come to you; go out and search for the person who has the knowledge and abilities to advise on one or more of the organization's strategic objectives.

- Inform the prospective board candidate that you want to meet to provide information about your organization and to see if there are mutual interests that could lead to a board position or other organizational involvement.

- Provide board prospects with a packet of materials that includes a board job description and pertinent information regarding a board member's participation, including the following:

    How many meetings a year are scheduled, and what is an acceptable number of absences (for example, "Board members are expected to attend 75 percent of all scheduled meetings")

    Whether board members are required to serve on committees

    Level of involvement in fundraising and other organizational events

    Requirements that board members make an annual financial contribution

To avoid potential conflicts of a personal or professional nature, it is important to inform the prospective board member about the organization's business relationships in the areas of banking, investments, and legal counsel. In addition, many board prospects are interested in liability protection and want to know whether the organization has directors' and officers' liability insurance coverage.

Each organization must develop its own set of written expectations and present the relevant information to board candidates during the prospecting stage. It is unfair for board members to learn what is expected of them on a trial-and-error basis following their election to the board. This negative way of welcoming board members will naturally serve as a powerful restraining force.

Candidates need to know what they are stepping into. It is not evenhanded, for example, for a new board member to learn that board meetings run five hours when two hours is all he or she has available. Under those circumstances, a reasonable person would not agree to serve. If someone is not told, agrees to serve, and then consistently leaves meetings early, other board members might view the new person as lacking in conscientiousness or commitment when the truth is that the person does care but that other obligations in life, such as commitments to family and work, take precedence over the board role.

Active Intervention

So what do you do if a new board member does not meet the expectations that were outlined and reviewed during the recruitment stage? Intervene right away with a first-order approach. If the new board member starts to miss meetings, contact the person and ask about his or her ability to participate as was outlined during recruitment. Intervening quickly sends a message that participation is important and that the organization insists on upholding the expectations that were outlined prior to being offered a position on the board.

If the intervention fails to spark the level of involvement that is expected, use a second-order approach such as exploring what type of help the board member could use to make effective fulfill-ment of the governing role more feasible. A nonthreatening discussion with the board member about his or her participation can be viewed as a positive expression of concern for the person's well-being. If appropriate, do not hesitate to invite the board member to take a leave of absence from the board if he or she is dealing with personal issues that will distract from active board involvement. By taking a supportive approach and providing an unexpected offer of a leave, you make it less likely that the board member will be defen-sive. Instead, the board member will see that he or she is regarded as an important asset to the organization. When this type of tone is set, the board member may either request a leave of absence or resign without the feeling of having failed. In either outcome, the nonprofit organization maintains a friend and supporter.

6

Cultural Depression in Nonprofit Organizations

The Problem

Organizational culture can be an extremely powerful force in the workplace. It can personify a spirit or tone that pervades the workplace and conveys the values of the nonprofit organization. Culture can cut both ways; it can be a tool that positively builds an organization, or it can lead to a morale problem and disorder. In fact, a dour milieu can impair an employee's perception of the organization and dampen staff members' loyalty to the organization and to their job duties.

When cultural depression is experienced on a wider scale, the workplace environment can be toxic, resulting in high staff turnover. Staff turnover ordinarily does not reflect a healthy condition, nor does it send a favorable message about the organization's being an attractive place to work. Turnover of staff leads to greater costs for recruitment and training. It can also hamper continuity of client services.

Organizational culture will develop on its own if managers and staff do not intentionally shape one. If unimpeded, individuals may not realize that they are engaging in patterns of behavior that are reinforcing cultural depression. By not seeing what role they play in the problem, managers may be inclined to attribute high staff turnover to emotional factors like staff burnout or circumstances that are external to the organization and beyond their control.

The Case Study

The following case study focuses on cultural depression as experienced by three nonprofit organizations. The organizations were selected for their differences—differences in nonprofit sector interests, organizational purpose, and geographical location. The common threads they shared were high rates of staff turnover as a result of cultural depression. Another similarity is their directors' response to questions about the cause for high staff turnover. None of the three managers considered the possibility that the organization's culture could be a contributing factor to the staff turnover problem.

I was initially introduced to the Mental Health Center of Dakota Creek, the Bakersville Boys' Ranch, and the Cardinal Art Museum of Design and Printing by a foundation that funds in the western region of the United States.

At the invitation of the funder, all three nonprofit organizations agreed to meet with me alone and also as a small discussion group. The topic of discussion was trying to fill staff vacancies. By all accounts, the three organizations were well respected in their communities and had a solid reputation for providing good services. Despite their first-rate public image, staff turnover was a major problem. In a period of one year, the Mental Health Center turned over more than 65 percent of its direct care staff, the boys' ranch experienced a 55 percent turnover, and the art museum was just slightly over 40 percent. Why were these three different types of nonprofit organizations experiencing difficulties in retaining staff?

In an interview about staff recruitment and retention, Bob Nelson, executive director of the Mental Health Center, explained the problem of high staff turnover as a result of the stressful nature of working in human services. In Bob's words, "High stress and low pay equal staff burnout."

Just outside of Albuquerque, New Mexico, Mary Trujillo, executive director of the Cardinal Art Museum, agreed to discuss her human resource issues. Mary was concerned that staff turnover was high, but she ascribed it to the museum's being located in a tourist center that competes heavily for labor. She explained that nonprofit employers struggle to keep staff because of the high cost of living in the area. She also stated that it was difficult to pay the same level of wages as the for-profit businesses in the area.

In rural Montana, the Bakersville Boys' Ranch is situated ten miles from its nearest neighbor. The boys come to the ranch from all over Montana through court-ordered referrals and from juvenile diversion programs in surrounding western states. Mick Werbach, the executive director of the boys' ranch describes the work as "intense but rewarding."

Mick attributed his organization's staff turnover to two factors: the ranch's rural location and emotional burnout. "It is painful to see the kids' families refusing to come and visit, and some are not interested in having their sons return home."

The three organizations made a commitment to work on their staff turnover issues because the ongoing replacement of employees represented a real loss in terms of both finances and time.

Analysis of the Case

Many problems present as primary issues but are not the primary problem. They are actually the symptoms of the primary problem, just as fever is the symptom of a greater problem such as a bacterial infection. In this case, the presenting problem was "high staff turnover."

Each executive director was able to articulate a thoughtful and perfectly reasonable explanation for the staff retention problems. More important to the analysis, these nonprofit managers attributed their human resource problems to external factors that were largely beyond their control. They portrayed their organizations as victims of the economy, involved in fierce competition for staff from a lower-wage labor pool, or competing for young professionals who would not command high starting salaries.

The Solution

With an ongoing procession of newly hired staff coming in and an equal number of staff leaving, the three nonprofit managers had no expectations that staff would demonstrate loyalty to their jobs and remain for several years. Instead, they anticipated that staff would be motivated to leave the nonprofit because of burnout, emotional letdown, or better career and job opportunities. In addition, the managers attributed two additional factors to the staff turnover problem: geographical location and competition for labor at a certain wage level.

The three executive directors and their nonprofit managers made assumptions about the character of their nonmanagement employees. Managers looked for patterns of employee behavior that bolstered and reflected the reality that the managers had constructed about these people. For example, whenever a staff member resigned from the job and severed ties with the nonprofit, it served to reinforce the manager's belief system about employee instability and lack of loyalty.

Supervisors were not inclined to become close to individual staff members. By remaining aloof and not being employee-centered, the managers ignored the use of incentives to recognize and honor the work of employees. In fact, the three executive directors did not see the need for protocols for rewarding employees beyond an annual performance appraisal. Organizational resources were not used to improve career growth options, and longevity was not present as an organizational value. Consequently, staff would not hold their jobs for any lengthy period.

First-Order or Second-Order Approach?

We already know that a first-order approach was repeatedly used but did not lead to problem resolution or organizational change. That approach consisted of recruiting and advertising for staff to fill vacant positions. From what we know about the dynamics of the presenting problem and the first-order change attempts that failed, a second-order change approach was warranted.

Had these directors had the knowledge and skill to proceed on their own, they could have developed and implemented their own second-order strategies. But they were unaware of approaches to problem resolution and planned change using second-order strategies.

Selecting Theories for Examining the Issues

Two theory areas seemed to fit best with the presenting problems: organizational culture theory and communication theory.

A number of existing organizational behavior theorists have implied that a link exists between employee performance and organizational culture. One theorist, Ralph Kilmann (1989, p. 50), for example, speaks of organizational culture as an "invisible force behind the tangible and observable in an organization, a social energy that moves people into action. Culture is to the organization what personality is to the individual—a hidden yet unifying theme that provides meaning, direction, and mobilization."

Relevant literature convinced me that we should consider the link between organizational culture and effective organizational performance in these three nonprofit organizations. We began to closely examine each organization's stated and practiced values, staffing practices, norms, basic assumptions, ethical considerations, and processes used for formal and informal decision making. Three ideas emerged:

1. Organizational culture may need to be changed if the nonprofit organization is experiencing problems with staff loyalty.

2. An organization's culture establishes the boundaries of peer interaction and how individuals are either included or excluded from work teams and social groups.

3. Inconsistent treatment of personnel can lead to cultural depression.

In addition to exploring organizational culture issues, it seemed that the nonprofit managers in these three organizations might have been contributing to the problem through a process of verbal and nonverbal communication. Communication theory, and specifically the concept of metacommunication (a secondary message that is sent simultaneously with a content message), suggests the possibility that managers were subtly conveying their expectations that the new employee would not stay long. Such messages are hidden in the verbal messages sent by the managers. The metamessage can be conveyed by tone of voice, placing an emphasis on a word, or using double entendre, making it unclear which meaning was meant for the new employee.

Accepting the likelihood that metamessages were being conveyed, consciously or not, we also considered the applicability of attribution theory and social perception theory. These two theories were helpful in explaining how the nonprofit managers in the three organizations went about characterizing their new employees in stereotypical ways. Through these lenses, we could see that the managers sought out causes of the behavior they saw in employees who worked for less than a year or two. These managers used attribution processes as a way of predicting the short-term stays of their employees. Once the managers formulated the idea that most employees were not going to demonstrate long-term loyalty to the nonprofit, the managers made quick judgments about each new employee and integrated attributions to form an impression about each new employee. In fact, such first impressions are so tenacious that the fact that the managers' perceptions might be incorrect never even occurs to them. This staunch view may explain why the three executive directors were able to describe with conviction their beliefs about the causes of their organizations' high staff turnover.

Formulating a Hypothesis to Guide Planned Change

If the diagnostic assessment is correct, the hypothesis that will be tested is that high staff turnover is the result of cultural depression.

Furthermore, if we can come up with an intervention that is able to address and ameliorate the condition of cultural depression, staff turnover rates will improve. We also assume that the cultural depression is being reinforced by the social perceptions and attributions that the managers make upon the arrival of their newly hired employees or even at the time of interviewing job candidates.

Devising an Alternative Intervention Strategy Based on the Hypothesis

When designing an intervention strategy, it is important to consider the type of outcome we want to achieve and what would constitute success. It would not be realistic to think that our intervention could completely eliminate staff turnover. Some amount of staff turnover is expected as a natural phenomenon in organizational systems. People will eventually leave an organization, because of illness, relocation, retirement, career opportunities, or death. So even though turnover will continue, slowing or reducing the rate of staff turnover would be one measure of a successful intervention.

Identifying the likely target for an intervention strategy, as well as eliminating targets, is a vital task in the design process. In this case, the planned change effort has to counter the natural forces that lead to stagnation. Kilmann (1989, p. 55) suggests that "if left alone, all cultures eventually become dysfunctional." Strategic decisions about maintaining or changing an organization's culture should not be taken lightly. Before moving forward with an intervention strategy, it is important to recognize that once a second-order intervention strategy is launched, the structure and normality of the organization will be challenged.

Systems theory provides some explanation or insight into the unpredictable response that any intervention can trigger. An intervention in one area will cause a ripple throughout the organization. An intervention in one area will lead to changes in other areas, whether we planned for changes in those areas or not.

For this reason, before calculating a second-order intervention, the three executive directors were encouraged to discuss the topic of organizational culture at their next board and management team meetings. These discussions focused on the design and development of a new organizational culture. Changing organizational culture requires retaining the best of the organization's way of life and integrating it into a unifying vision or mission in which the staff, managers, and board members can rally.

To initiate a change in a nonprofit organization's culture leading to an improvement of staff recruitment and retention, the executive directors and their senior managers first had to accept the idea, or at least the possibility, that their organizational problems were highly relevant to their organization's internal environment. They need to confront one of *Pogo*'s well-known revelations: "We have met the enemy and he is us."

Focusing on the internal environment does not discount the possibility that some problems may be the result of impinging forces from the external environment. These externally generated issues also need to be addressed. Focusing the change effort on the organization's culture allows the organization's decision makers to design a blueprint for addressing these complex issues.

Because of our belief that the managers were acting in specific ways toward their new employees as a result of social perceptions and attributions, the use of contingency management models was considered in the design of an intervention plan. Contingency models can target workplace culture by either matching a manager to a situation or having a manager alter his or her supervisory style to fit employee needs. Through these contingency efforts, managers can influence and increase staff satisfaction, productivity, and longevity with the organization (Fielder, 1967; Hersey, Blanchard, and Johnson, 1996). Besides matching supervisors more closely to address the supervisory needs of the employees, we also included Kurt Lewin's Force Field Analysis ideas. Conceptually, this meant that we wanted to reduce or immobilize the forces that were restricting staff commitment to the organization and improve managers' commitment to staff development.

Implementing the New Strategy

To produce cultural change in their nonprofit organizations, the three organizational leaders needed to develop a stronger commitment to the process of change than maintaining the status quo. Successful change efforts require individual introspection and some emotional discomfort, and therefore the organizations' executive directors must not equivocate about their intentions to create change. They must demonstrate their willingness to bear any personal and professional discomfort that can be part of the change experience. If the organizational leaders cannot demonstrate this level of commitment, their staff will be even less likely to accept the changes. For these reasons, I asked the three directors to pledge their commitment to a cultural change effort before taking any further steps.

Once the leaders of the three organizations had pledged to engage in an organization culture change effort, I asked them to communicate their pledge to their staff. I informed each of the executive directors that they should anticipate a reaction of fear and panic among their staff. It is natural for staff to fear that a reorganization will mean the loss of jobs. Consequently, I advised the directors to focus on two major points when informing their staff of the impending change in culture: first, that many staff members will experience a range of emotional reactions to the announcement, all perfectly normal, and second, that staff can contribute a great deal by becoming involved in shaping the new organization. When staff are made part of the change process, their fears can be converted into positive change efforts.

Sharing this information with the staff is an important demonstration of concern and of understanding the human factor. I told the directors that their statements might also give each staff member a sense of comfort that the executive director understands the process of change.

One of our planned objectives was to identify and increase the driving forces that could promote staff retention. To begin reducing the restraining forces and increase the driving forces, I recommended that each organization hold an open meeting with its staff at least once a week. During these all-staff meetings, the directors and their managers were to encourage discussion of various rumors, such as staff changes, termination, or anything else that seemed important.

Forecasting uncomfortable feelings will not cause those uncomfortable reactions to occur. Staff will experience anxiety and hear many rumors without any management participation. But forecasting these symptoms gains control of the restraining forces that might otherwise disrupt the change process. Because reactions were predicted, when staff members experience feelings of anxiety, say, or hear rumors, these are treated as natural responses to the change process and not as dysfunctional reactions.

Having taken these appropriate actions, the executive director will be seen as an individual who understands organizational dynamics. Consequently, staff should have more confidence in the change process and be more receptive to the objectives that the executive director and senior managers are trying to accomplish. Such reactions enhance the driving forces toward successful change. As the restraining forces diminish, staff will have an opportunity to adjust emotionally and cognitively to the reality that organizational change will occur and will actively participate in the process.

To advance the change efforts, one of the behavioral leadership theories that is an advantageous tool to use is Likert's management systems model (1961, 1967). The approach suggests that if management is employee-centered and demonstrates trust and confidence in its employees, it will be rewarded with motivated employees who will gladly work alongside management to support the mission of the organization. Implementation activities of Likert's model includes regularly scheduled all-staff meetings in which the executive director discusses his or her vision for the new organizational culture and invites staff reactions and dialogue. Some staff members may share the executive director's vision and openly express their support. Generally, when staff participate in these types of meetings, managers will discover leaders among the staff who can be helpful in promoting the new organizational vision.

Since the conveyance of trust is an important factor in Likert's management systems model, an appropriate integration of a first-order change strategy may include the development of a staff advisory committee. The committee would need to be given a clear set of directives that are focused and potentially productive. One of the committee's charges should be to invite and represent the viewpoints of the employees. In this way, staff would have a formalized voice and a mechanism to provide feedback to management.

The formation of an advisory committee must be more than a symbolic gesture. The composition of the committee should include only individuals who genuinely seem attracted to the new culture and are willing to participate in the change process even if they have some minor concerns or reservations about experiencing an organizational change. Individuals who represent staff on the advisory committee will become natural ambassadors of the change effort. In this way, advisory committee members should be encouraged to invite discussion among their peers and periodically survey the staff's feelings and position on the change efforts through focus groups and "brown bag" lunch meetings.

Because management is sometimes viewed as aloof, it may be advantageous to discuss the problems and issues of the change effort with the staff advisory committee (and at the all-staff meetings). In the case studies, managers were encouraged to express their own doubts and anxieties about going through the change process. Some managers did share their feelings and thoughts about the change process. Other managers did not want to disclose their feelings even though they were told that it would be helpful for staff to hear them express their concerns.

When staff heard managers express their reservations about cultural change, some staff viewed the admission as a refreshing sign that a positive shift in culture was already under way. Some managers who had a reputation as being cold, self-righteous, and surly were for the first time viewed as sensitive and human.

Although some staff may have been suspicious of managers who suddenly became candid and interested in the views of staff, staff members did not challenge the authenticity of their managers' feelings about these issues. The shift in the managers' position and its acceptance by staff may be the result of reframing as staff came to view managers as sharing their own uncertainties. The recognition of this common bond moved staff to support their managers in the culture change effort.

One recognizable benefit of this culture change effort was the attention given to renewing the organizational vision. Participation in a discussion of vision, values, and beliefs was a new experience for most of the employees of all three nonprofit organizations. These discussions created positive excitement throughout each organization. According to development consultant Peter Block (1987, p. 103), "It is the dialogue about vision that helps us connect with each other in a way that matters. Our vision can, at times, be a source of conflict, but more often it is a source of connection."

Articulating a new organizational vision was a cleansing ritual. Each nonprofit organization had acknowledged that it had been weak and asked staff to partner and share in the activities to reinvigorate the organization. Once the shared vision was established, it was important to continue to build support among the staff, to enlighten them and to secure their commitment to share in the activities that supported the organization's vision. The values and beliefs associated with the vision directly tied to the organization's newly developing culture.

In fact, the development of a vision from the organization's top leadership was critical for shaping the organizational culture and setting the tone for a discussion about organizational goals and objectives. In many organizations, the vision that is articulated by the organization's executive director does not always filter down to all of the employees with the same strength and conviction. For this reason, the managers were asked to use the executive director's statements as a guide for each department, division, or team. Each of these units developed its own vision statement, consistent with or complementary to the vision statement outlined by the executive director. Finally, all of the organization's employees were encouraged to develop personal visions for their job, using the organization's vision as their foundation.

The Results

After twelve months, all three organizations reported significant improvements in staff retention. Two of the organizations also took the advice to initiate a staff satisfaction survey to further demonstrate management's interest in its staff. One of these two also developed a staff incentive system, giving rewards for staff achievements. The third organization is still considering its alternatives.

7

Political Performance

The Problem

Writing a chapter about political performance is an unpleasant task for the reason that it highlights the fact that some individuals are driven by their own personal gain and not by the altruistic intentions of the nonprofit organization that employs them. Political performance is the cause of many nonprofit organizational failures, but it has not received much attention in the literature.

Political performance refers to a set of specialized goal-directed behaviors that are generally self-serving. A focus on "doing good" for oneself without regard to the consequences of the nonprofit organization is not generally thought to be characteristic behavior for employees of nonprofit organizations. "Swimming with the sharks" is the metaphor applied to such behaviors in the for-profit sector. For some reason, we are generally not surprised when we hear of politically motivated behavior in for-profit organizations.

Acknowledging that political behavior can also occur in nonprofit organizations causes some cognitive dissonance. Rightly or wrongly, a cultural norm has evolved that distinguishes the behavior of organizations that focus on the bottom line from those that focus on mission and charity. This explains at least in part the perceived unexpectedness of political performance behaviors in nonprofit organizations.

Political performance behaviors almost always consist of efforts to acquire and use power in order to influence decisions that will benefit the political performer. When nonprofit managers exhibit political performance behaviors, they usually target individuals in subordinate positions. Individuals who are targeted frequently feel powerless, ill treated, and exploited.

Although political behavior can exist in all types and sizes of nonprofit organizations, some political behaviors are considered natural and others less so. Natural political behavior is inherent in certain organizational positions that require the use of authority. Managerial and supervisory positions often entail responsibilities to direct or judge other employees' work efforts. In some cases, even the most consensus-driven style managers must rely on their position of power and make decisions they believe to be in the best interest of the organization. This use of natural and positional power is carried out to reach departmental or organizational objectives that favor the nonprofit organization.

In the expression "political performance," the reference does not encompass natural or position-related power. Rather, it refers to the type of organizational politics that is intended to benefit the political performer. Power of this kind is neither sanctioned nor legitimate. Consequently, it can poison the work environment.

Note that it is possible to possess forms of power that are individually based but not attributable to one's position. For example, an individual can be very influential or considered powerful as a result of having certain skills, abilities, or knowledge that others may not possess.

The Case Study

The following two case examples were selected because they each illustrate political performance. The differences in the two organizations also demonstrate how political performance can surface in almost any nonprofit organization because the issues are personality-driven, not organizationally inspired or dependent on a particular type of nonprofit organization.

These case studies are unique because unlike the key players in other chapters, the two individuals who had the presenting problems are neither executive directors nor board members. Because I was asked to provide help but not brought in by the top brass, I needed to avoid an ethical dilemma. For this reason, I did not design the interventions or actively consult on these two cases; my involvement was strictly educational.

I knew Jack casually during the days when he was completing a postdoctoral project at the university where I taught, and Beth is a relative of one of my colleagues. The issues that they both presented had similar overtones from a political performance standpoint, although their requests for help came three years apart. In each case, I told them that the best I could do to help them was to provide education about organizational dynamics that would cover their work-related issues. The agreement included an understanding that they would make their own decisions about designing and implementing an intervention approach. In both cases, my offer required that Jack and Beth enroll as nondegree students in my graduate-level course on nonprofit organizational behavior and change. There were about twenty other students in Jack's class and in Beth's. Students were encouraged to use the course as an opportunity to examine their own organizational experiences for classroom discussion and homework assignments. Also, students were asked to share opinions, make suggestions, and give feedback on any of the organizational issues that their classmates shared.

Beth and the Performing Arts Center

Beth was a senior accountant with a nonprofit performing arts center. Like many nonprofits in the performing arts, money had been tight for years. Rather than cancel performances as funds diminished, the board of directors chose to downsize staff, expanding job responsibilities without additional compensation.

For three years, Beth's supervisor, Stewart Clarkson, the chief financial officer (CFO), had been promising her an increase in pay that would bring her closer to the salary levels being paid for similar positions in nearby nonprofit organizations. Given her role, Beth knew that money was tight, but she also knew that the organization could easily afford to pay her $4,000 more per year.

Stewart had adeptly engaged in political performance behaviors for many years. The following example illustrates their routine. One or two days after Beth and Stewart had a discussion about her financial needs, Stewart reported "bad news" that the executive director rejected Stewart's request for Beth to receive a pay increase. Whether Stewart actually advocated on Beth's behalf was left unclear.

As CFO of the organization, Stewart was the only senior manager, along with the executive director, who regularly met with the board of directors and its executive committee. If we were to speculate about Stewart's motives, we might say that his personal goal was to demonstrate his competency and keen financial acumen to the board of directors. He spoke of himself as being a tightfisted manager and frequently made note of his commitment to the board and the organization. A review of the organization's tax records for the prior five years revealed that Stewart managed to secure an annual salary increase for himself and for the executive director in each of those years. If not for Beth's skills and knowledge, Stewart might not have the excellent financial reports that he shared with the board. He, of course, received the compliments for her work.

Beth finally gathered up the courage to give Stewart an ultimatum: either get her a $4,000 increase, or she would leave the organization. As usual, Stewart claimed to have fought very hard for her and was able to secure a $3,000 increase. Without another job to go to, Beth was in no financial position to quit and walk out. She accepted the increase.

Jack and the Institute for the Advancement
of Academic Freedom

The Institute for the Advancement of Academic Freedom is a non-profit "think tank" with close associations to institutions of higher education in the Rocky Mountain region of the United States. The institute is funded principally by government grants and private foundations.

Jack is the director of research, and he reports to the institute's executive director, Dillon Rice. The institute employs ten of the brightest minds in academia. Jack is considered the number two person in the organization and the likely successor when Dillon Rice retires.

Jack is well compensated, and his salary is a major motivator for staying on the job. On the other hand, Dillon earns at least twice what he pays Jack. Dillon has a reputation as a savvy entrepreneur and is a charming and witty man who can talk his way into a contract if given the chance to get in front of funders. Whatever project promises he makes, he expects that Jack will figure out a way to get the job done and well within the budget. Dillon relies on Jack because he does not have the research background to do the work himself. While Dillon does open the doors to opportunities, he has never written any of the proposals or grant progress reports. In fact, he has not participated in the writing of several journal articles in which he has insisted on being listed as coauthor or lead author. Given the reputation of the institute and the number of articles that have been published by its staff, Dillon has gained various honors and served as the chair of various professional society boards and committees.

Jack told Dillon that taking credit for written contributions that he did not write was intellectually dishonest and that he would not allow Dillon's name to be added to any of his work products again. Dillon replied that Jack was a "big boy" and could go along for the ride or walk out the door and never look back.

Jack could not just walk away. He had a family with two children in college and knew that his current level of compensation would be hard to replace. Also, his family balked at the idea of moving out of state or to another city. In addition, Dillon made it harder for Jack to leave by providing Jack with a company-leased vehicle and a monthly allowance for its upkeep. With Jack's son commuting to college, the family was in need of another car. Access to a company car relieved Jack of a considerable logistical and financial burden. At age forty-seven, Jack was a very unhappy man but felt trapped intellectually, ethically, and economically.

Analysis of the Case

As presenting problems, Beth's and Jack's concerns were similar. Independently, they described their relationship with their immediate supervisors as strained. They felt intimidated, manipulated, and insecure.

Jack and Beth each painted a picture of dependency on their supervisors, although they did not like the way they were treated. They also stated that they could not trust their supervisor and were uncertain whether their supervisor was being truthful.

In analyzing political performance, it is important to clarify the placement and use of power in organizational relationships. One form of power that is based on organizational position and carries legitimate privileges to make decisions is having authority. Both Stewart Clarkson and Dillon Rice have authority to make decisions as a result of their management position in the organization.

Often the concept of leadership is defined as having power to influence the behavior of others. However, a distinction should be made between leadership influence and behavior that is based on political performance. Neither Stewart nor Dillon has exercised leadership. Beth and Jack are not followers as a result of their beliefs in the leadership of their supervisors. The power that comes from being a genuine leader is a result of the followers' beliefs in the person. Followers generally feel respected and believe in the vision of their leader. Should followers withdraw their support, the leader would not have influence over them. In the case of Beth and Jack, they followed and complied with their supervisors' wishes in response to feelings of fear and intimidation, not followership.

The Solution

The supervisory relationship between Stewart and Beth is built on Stewart's political performance practices. Plainly speaking, Stewart uses his relationship with his subordinate to advance his own standing in the organizational hierarchy. For example, he tells Beth that he is her advocate and will fight to help her get a raise. We can assume that his objective is to get Beth to feel grateful and work harder for him. The better her work products, the more competent he looks to the executive director and board members.

Stewart also uses the clout of intimidation with Beth. He knows that she is a single parent and not in a financial position to simply quit and walk away. He knows Beth's vulnerability and uses it to his advantage. In this case, Stewart also tries to isolate Beth from others in the organization by telling her to promise not to let everyone else know how he fights to improve her salary and position.

Stewart also uses intimidation when he grants Beth only $3,000 of the $4,000 that she anticipated and counted on for helping her meet her family and financial obligations. Adding an additional $1,000 to Beth's salary would not harm the organization, but by giving it to Beth, Stewart would be empowering and reinforcing her assertiveness. He does not want Beth to believe that she has an ability to make demands on him and succeed. By not giving her what he easily could, he keeps her feeling dejected and dependent on him. Although she does not receive the level of increase she wanted, she is still made to believe that Stewart is her champion.

In Jack's attempt to modify some of Dillon's political power practices, he takes a stand and tells Dillon that he will no longer be able to take credit for Jack's intellectual property. Unfortunately, Jack did not realize the futility in confronting someone who relies heavily on political performance and unprincipled practices. Individuals who knowingly engage in unethical activities to aggrandize their personal position in life very rarely feel guilt about their practices of intimidation and deception. In this case, Dillon responds with intimidation tactics to keep Jack subordinated. He tells Jack that he is a "big boy," first making an illusion to Jack as childlike and naïve. He also challenges Jack by suggesting that he should quit if he finds Dillon's behavior objectionable. Dillon's challenge to Jack is a classic reaction when an intimidator believes that his or her authority is being challenged. Argyris and Schön (1995) describe Dillon's type of reaction as skirting issues, attacking others, and escalating games of camouflage and deception. In this situation, Dillon is confident that Jack will not walk away from his job, so he escalates Jack's position of helplessness. Dillon fully knows of Jack's economic bind and has in fact helped structure Jack's salary and benefits to foster dependency in order to make it difficult for Jack to leave the institute. Instead of reacting to his outrage over Dillon's challenge to quit, Jack succumbs and feels even more powerless.

First-Order or Second-Order Approach?

It is quite common for individuals who have been victims of political performance to reach a boiling point when they finally react and take a stand on their own behalf. That is what Beth did by issuing an ultimatum for a $4,000 raise and what Jack did by telling Dillon that he could no longer put his name on Jack's intellectual products. These straightforward demands are typical of a first-order approach.

Unfortunately, when dealing with political performers, first-order approaches rarely succeed over the long term. The intervention might stave off political performer behaviors momentarily, but the effect usually doesn't last, and the original pattern of behavior returns.

However, occasionally first-order interventions achieve what appear to be longer-term successes. Usually this type of success happens by a stroke of luck whereby the (first-order) intervention produced some obvious benefits for the political performer. In those situations, the political performer is not responding to the needs of the individual who is making the demands but rather is responding to the parts that will yield some personal benefit.

In my experience, second-order interventions succeed more frequently. One of the challenges in developing a second-order approach to counter political performance behavior is to refrain from wanting to retaliate or seek retribution. Although this is a normal human response, ethical considerations come into play in an organizational context. Although some of the most powerful change strategies "use fire to fight fire," it is generally wise, unless one is advanced in dealing with political adversaries, to avoid using political performance to neutralize performance behaviors. One reason for avoiding these tactics is that your opponent is far more skilled and experienced in management by intimidation and manipulation than you are. Consequently, I refrain from teaching students to roll up their sleeves and use street-fighting tactics.

Selecting Theories for Examining the Issues

Political performance problems crop up in nonprofit organizations when power is concentrated in the wrong hands. Individuals who knowingly engage in political performance behaviors are sometimes referred to as having a Machiavellian personality, named for Niccolò Machiavelli, the sixteenth-century author of *The Prince*. Machiavelli's treatise was on the purposeful use of power and deceptive tactics. Individuals with a Machiavellian personality will use any means to achieve a desired end. Individuals who are organizationally ruthless have either a keenly honed or an innate understanding of organizational control tactics. They know, for example, how to present arguments that sound like they are marshaling support for the organization and on behalf of particular individuals when in reality their motives are for self-interest.

Stewart's and Dillon's abuses of power seem to model Machiavellianism. Individuals who have this personality characteristic tend to be pragmatic and can maintain emotional distance from the individuals they influence. Their credo would be something like "The ends justify the means—especially if the ends benefit me!"

Machiavellian personalities also seem to have a capacity for convincing their victims that the victims could not survive without them. This "one-up and one-down" relationship can be illustrated with the formula "The greater one's dependency is on A, the greater the power A has over B" (Robbins, 1998, p. 400). As long as Jack and Beth stay dependent on their supervisors and are fearful about breaking ties with them, Stewart will maintain control over Beth, and Dillon will have control over Jack.

Another lens to use to examine these relationships is through the power theories of French and Raven (1959). French and Raven were pioneer organizational behavior researchers who described the basis of "coercive power" as creating dependency through fear. Individuals who succumb to this form of power do so out of either physiological or safety needs. In this case, the supervisors manipulate Beth's and Jack's dependency on their salaries.

A counterpart of coercive power is "reward power." In addition to their ability to take away Beth's and Jack's livelihood, Dillon and Stewart also have the capacity to manipulate them by issuing rewards such as salary increases, new benefits, and promotions. In this case, Stewart dangles hope in front of Beth with a salary increase, and Dillon provides Jack with a company vehicle to further undermine Jack's efforts to become independent.

Formulating a Hypothesis to Guide Planned Change

Once Beth and Jack question the premise of their relationships with their aggressors, the door will wedge open for possible change.

Howard Nigel (1966) refers to this type of consciousness raising in "The Theory of Metagames," stating that individuals can choose to free themselves of their behaviors once they come to know and comprehend a theory about those behaviors.

Ashby (1956) states a similar assumption in his *Introduction to Cybernetics*, stating that how one gets one's own way is based on a foundation of the theories of games and cybernetics. In this situation, the hypothesis that we will come up with is based on game theory. By using the analogy that Beth's and Jack's situation is structured like a game, it suggests that rule awareness can play a decisive role in the outcome of that game.

In other words, by applying game theory, it would be possible for Beth and Jack to gain an understanding of the rules that have kept them trapped and dependent. Thereafter, they will have more freedom to choose their own movements. Their decision options will be either to play by the old rules or to try to establish a new set of rules.

Devising an Alternative Intervention Strategy Based on the Hypothesis

Watzlawick, Weakland, Fisch, and Erickson (1974) have promoted the concept of reframing as a therapeutic tool to help individuals stop engaging in self-defeating behaviors. I have found their concept of reframing to be extremely effective in approaching the design and implementation of second-order interventions.

Consequently, I believe that reframing is an important concept that should be taught to students of nonprofit organizational behavior. For this reason, a homework assignment I gave the students in my nonprofit organizational behavior and change courses was to "experience the effects of reframing." This exercise proved to be a powerful learning experience for Beth and for Jack, as well as for many other students over the years. Although my students typically engaged in this exercise because I assigned it, it is the type of activity that an individual who is knowledgeable of planned change techniques can readily design and self-prescribe.

The Homework Assignment

Students are informed that they have a homework assignment that will help them understand the concepts of political performance. They are also told that the assignment will help them understand how reframing, as a tool for a second-order intervention, might be used to facilitate planned change. As part of the instructions, students are asked to select two time periods a day when they will be able to spend no less than ten but no more than fifteen uninterrupted minutes on five consecutive days. It is preferable that the time be split between morning and evening hours and to the extent that is possible to begin the exercise at the same time of day on all five days. Once students have written down the time of day for their homework, the remainder of their assignment is read to them. They are told to listen to the following statement:

> The ability to take control of one's life in an organization may require engaging in self-protection and preservation, especially when a person is the target of inappropriate uses of power and authority. Taking some action is an important decision area for an individual who feels victimized by political power. If systems theory holds true, then by taking some action directed at correcting faulty uses of power and authority, some type of change will occur throughout the organization.
>
> You are to imagine that you are employed in a nonprofit organization. One day you are surprised by the revelation that you are a target of inappropriate uses of power and authority. You realize that your aggressor benefits at your personal or professional expense (or both).
>
> For each ten- to fifteen-minute period, imagine how the political performer interacts with you, to the other person's advantage. Select all relevant political performer approaches that were discussed in class and in your reading, especially the various political behaviors identified by Peter Block in *The Empowered Manager* (1997).

Implementing the New Strategy

The homework assignment was my intervention in helping my students understand the various uses of power. Normally, when one is the target of political performance behaviors, one's response is generally an emotional one. By reacting emotionally and not being clearheaded, it would be difficult to break down the components of an interactional game in which one is a participant. In order to understand the patterns and the rules that are inherent in an interaction "game" of political performance, the assignment provided a structure for students to safely examine a variety of manipulative tactics that have been used on them and others.

The Results

Through the exercise, Beth became aware of the pattern of behavior that she and Stewart engage in and decided to intervene with her own second-order approach. Rather than rely on the existing rules where Stewart is in the role of champion but also reinforcing Beth's dependency, Beth consciously altered one of the trigger behaviors common to her relationship with Stewart. She told Stewart that she wanted to have a meeting with the executive director to discuss her recent raise. Stewart indicated that that would not be a good move for her career, coming across as defensive, demanding, and angry. Beth assured him that her motive for the meeting was not to complain but rather to personally thank the executive director for the salary increase. Stewart offered to pass along her message the next time he met with the executive director. But Beth was persistent and reframed Stewart's attempt to restrain her by expressing her appreciation to Stewart for trying to be "so helpful and protective." She then modified the rules of the game by suggesting that the two of them attend the appointment with the executive director. Because of her doggedness to meet with the executive director, Stewart realized that it was to his advantage to at least attend the meeting. When they did meet, Beth expressed her appreciation for the raise and wanted the chance to directly express her feelings of gratitude directly to both Stewart and the executive director. Another rule change occurred by this demonstration: Beth did not need Stewart to be her ambassador to the executive director.

Flattered by Beth's gracious statements, the executive director responded that his was an "open door" and that she should feel free to make an appointment at any time. The outcome was better than Beth had anticipated. By changing some of the rules of the inter-active game, Beth felt liberated. She was in control of her own fate and did not need to be as dependent on Stewart as she had been.

The course assignment also helped Jack examine the interplay between himself and Dillon. Jack recognized that Dillon actually depended on him for increasing Dillon's own professional standing. Jack reframed his position of weakness to a position of strength. Unfortunately, Jack did not use his reframing as part of a second-order strategy. Instead, driven by his own feelings of anger, he engaged in some political behaviors. Jack called a meeting of the institute staff and told all of them that if Dillon wanted to place his name on any of their written work, they should make him pay for it through some form of bartering. He advised everyone that they should ask for more money, time off, or additional benefits. Jack tried using the metaphor of Dillon as not a manufacturer but a buyer of goods and services who should therefore not be portrayed as the originator of the goods.

Instead of modifying the rules of the game using a second-order approach, Jack resorted to a first-order position and retaliated against Dillon. Needless to say, Dillon was furious when he heard about Jack's meeting with the staff. Recognizing that he could not trust Jack's behavior and fearing that Jack would incite the staff against him, Dillon fired Jack.

Interestingly, even with his employment termination, Jack claimed to feel liberated and empowered by his first-order actions. He predicted that his (political) intervention of bringing the staff together would lead to some (rule) changes at the institute, although he would not directly benefit from them. Jack had recognized how much Dillon needed him for reputation building, but rather than use that information to modify the rules of their interactions, he created a situation that left Dillon without much choice but to sever their ties.

An Alternative Approach

Under other circumstances, I would have liked to provide some counsel to Jack before he took the steps to call a meeting with staff and rally them against Dillon. It does seem that Jack's way of handling his anger was "passive-aggressive," a label used to describe a person's expression of hostility through indirect communication. Some people find it is a difficult or scary task to tell another person that they are feeling upset and angry with the person and then take appropriate action to resolve the anger. Instead of being direct in their expression of anger, they channel their expression through symbolic and nonverbal means of communication, and sometimes they will even find ways to get other people to express anger and hostility for them.

When a person suppresses feelings, it is not uncommon for there to be a rebound effect, affecting the person's own feelings of lack of confidence, low self-esteem, unhappiness, and depression. For that reason, it would be difficult for Jack to accept a first-order recommendation that required him to directly express his feelings of anger to Dillon and then quit. Instead, as we have seen, it was safer for Jack to express his anger indirectly and provoke Dillon into firing him.

Nevertheless, since I am not in the business of providing psychotherapy to Jack, my initial approach would be a straightforward first-order approach consisting of a conversation with Jack. I would ask Jack about his fears of leaving the institute. Is it really the money? Is it really his family holding him back? Or is it the pervasive fear of the unknown?

If Jack asked what I would do in his situation, I would not hold back; a first-order reply would be direct and to the point. I would tell him that I would resign if I were in his shoes, and I would urge him to resign as soon as possible. I would also advise him that he needs to make firm decisions about how he should comport himself with Dillon and also decide when and under what terms he will leave the institute. The overarching goal would be to incite Jack to take control and not behave in passive ways that lead others to make the key decisions that have a direct bearing on his life.

If there were simply no sign that Jack was taking charge of his life decisions and if he continued to express ambivalence—whether his excuses were tied to money, a company car, or other items that conveniently help Jack avoid direct decision making—the next step would be a second-order approach. For the development of a second-order approach, I would rely on the same personality and communication theories that helped me gain an understanding of Jack's behaving and coping mechanisms.

In a second-order approach, I would explain to Jack that I appreciate how difficult it is to make such weighty life and career decisions. I would apologize to Jack for what might have appeared to be my being pushy in urging him to make a decision. I would tell him that my intentions were good, but I could see that I might not have been very helpful since I really do not know what it is like to be "in his shoes." I would encourage Jack not to be hasty in making decisions until he really felt safe, confident, and in control.

By stating an apology and making alternative recommendations to Jack, I would be stepping out of the contentious role that I had placed myself in during the earlier first-order attempt. I refer to the experience as being "contentious" because any suggestion I would have made that he had not followed would mean that we disagreed with each other on how to handle his situation. During the first-order discussions, I would likely have been perceived as not being helpful or empathic. By apologizing, I would consciously be taking a "one-down" position, thus relieving Jack of the pressure of not following my advice.

The objective of a second-order approach would be to reframe Jack's indecision as really a struggle of giving up his role of protecting the institute's reputation and his loyalty to help Dillon. That type of statement is designed to cause a shift in Jack's thinking. It is one thing for Jack to think that Dillon's career is advanced by Jack's being bullied and threatened; it is quite another to face the idea that he is choosing to protect Dillon's welfare and professional standing. Thinking of himself as Dillon's protector would be such an untenable situation, I would expect Jack to resign and let Dillon pick up the pieces.

In summary, the opportunity to have engaged in an alternative approach and avoid the more-of-the-same failure must take into account the views, personality style, and expectations of those whose problems are to be changed. Reframing might have given Jack a different view of the forces that kept him from changing. If so, he would have the opportunity to alter the rules and make obsolete the interpersonal game that he had habitually engaged in that prevented him from facing change. The very elements that prevented change in the past are used to bring about change in this alternative form of intervention.

8

Role Confusion

The Problem

The most prevalent question that I have encountered over the past two decades is "What are the duties of a nonprofit board of directors, and how does its role and responsibilities differ from those of an executive director?"

If this question were as simple to answer as it appears, first-order exercises would have provided a satisfactory solution by now, and this question would be a thing of the past. The identification of job duties is not the core issue of role ambiguity. The issue is actually a complex human resource management problem in which there is a breakdown in the process of communicating task assignments and responsibilities and clarifying work and performance expectations. This communication breakdown is typically associated with receiving too little, too much, or contradictory information about one's role in an organization or with a board member's inadequate processing or assimilation of the information received.

One recognizable example of role confusion is when an individual learns that he or she has overstepped assigned job responsibilities (or what was thought to be job responsibilities) and encroached on the workload and responsibilities of other employees or volunteers. Role confusion also occurs when an individual is given work directives that he or she does not believe to be appropriate to his or her position in the organization.

When role confusion occurs, others may register annoyance, anger, disappointment, or frustration at seeing a colleague performing job duties inappropriately. Spending an unusual amount of time thinking about and questioning another person's work obligations could be another symptom of role confusion. When someone in an organization perseverates about another's job performance or lack of performance, it is important to consider that what is at issue may not be an intentional avoidance of job responsibilities or a lack of competency but rather a lack of adequate knowledge about role-specific job functions and performance expectations. Because the organizational and human resource stakes are high, there is good reason to be concerned when ambiguity exists in nonprofit organizations. Uncertainty about what board members, committee members, and executive management staff should be doing in their respective nonprofit organizational roles will likely lead to organizational conflict and stress among the individuals involved. Ultimately, role confusion in nonprofit organizations translates into poor services and mission failure.

The Case Study

The mission of the Morgan Beach County Seniors Campaign is "to improve the quality of living for senior citizens of Morgan Beach County." Generally known as just "the Campaign," the organization has a robust reputation and often receives requests for testimony in support of or against potential legislation. The Campaign also participates in several legislative coalitions of interest to senior and retired citizens.

David Bauer accepted the appointment of chairperson of the organization's prestigious governmental affairs committee (GAC). With David's background as a retired policy analyst for a large state legislature and as a former lobbyist for one of the big lobbying firms in the capital, chairing the GAC seemed like a perfect fit. David was also the Campaign's representative on a medical care coalition that focuses on medical services and medical insurance issues.

At one of the medical care coalition meetings, after David accepted the role of GAC chair for the Campaign, a state senator was invited to discuss the development of a bill that would give tax incentives for hospitals, local medical clinics, and physicians in private medical practices that provide at least 15 percent of their services to low-income and indigent citizens in need of emergency medical care. When the discussion shifted to the amount of the fiscal note (that is, the costs to the state in lost tax revenue) associated with a new tax credit, David took that opportunity to announce that the Senior Campaign wholeheartedly supported the effort and would lobby to have the state redirect existing financial subsidies of nursing home facilities to underwrite the costs of implementing these new tax credits.

The executive director of the Morgan Beach Association of Nursing Home Administrators (MBANHA), a coalition member, called Jane McGrath, the Senior Campaign's executive director, to express outrage at this unexpected announcement. Jane was equally shocked to learn of this development when she received a call from the *Morgan Beach Daily News*, seeking a statement about the Campaign's anti–nursing home funding stance. Jane soon telephoned David and told him he should not speak on behalf of the Campaign without first discussing this with other board members.

Within two days after Jane's call to David, the Campaign's board chair, Karen Kelman, called Jane to share a complaint received from David and his committee. The substance of the complaint was that Jane was unappreciative of the committee's work and acted rudely and condescendingly during a phone call to David about a statement he had made at the coalition meeting. At David's incitement, several committee members questioned whether they should resign if the committee's motives were going to be severely questioned.

Karen directed Jane to fix and repair the degrading relationship with the MBANHA and the medical care coalition. Jane was further directed to tell the MBANHA that the Senior Campaign would be glad to meet to discuss the policy position articulated by

David. Karen also asked Jane to resolve the volunteers' concerns about not feeling respected.

Jane responded defensively, expressing her concerns that she was being blamed and held accountable for the internal and external relationship problems triggered by David's actions. According to Jane, she had only informed David that his policy statement would need to be discussed at the next board meeting.

Karen was dissatisfied with Jane's display of hostility and recommended that the executive committee take disciplinary action against Jane for "insubordination." Karen was also troubled that this was not the first incident of a volunteer who autocratically represented a policy position in a public meeting without the position having first undergone a review and formal sanctioning by the board of directors. Karen suggested that Jane should have developed a process to prevent these situations from arising. Also, it was not the first time that volunteers either threatened or actually quit because they felt unappreciated by Jane and her staff.

Jane quit in protest after receiving the written disciplinary warning from Karen and the executive committee. In her resignation letter, Jane stated that she was not responsible for the misguided actions of the volunteers and declared that the board chair and board members should be held accountable. Jane cited other instances of volunteers taking unauthorized policy actions during the period she was the deputy director, "working under the former executive director." Following those critical events, "Karen and the former executive director should have taken some leadership responsibility to protect the board's interests" by developing a set of rules or guidelines for volunteers. Karen retorted that to her knowledge, the board had not seen the need to take any disciplinary action against the former executive director.

Analysis of the Case

Apparently, Jane's resignation letter did have some impact on the board of directors. Consequently, the executive committee requested help and characterized the presenting problem as "needing some direction in three areas." The first need was to prevent volunteers from representing their personal views as policy decisions of the Senior Campaign, unless the board had actually adopted the policy; second was to ensure that volunteers are satisfied with their volunteer assignments; and third was to make a good choice in the selection of a new executive director.

The Senior Campaign's presenting problem, at face value, appears to be relatively benign. However, we should keep in mind that organizational representatives commonly downplay issues and portray their presenting problems as not being severe, merely in need of a little tweaking, when in reality their organization may be quite dysfunctional and about to explode or implode. There is usually no conscious effort made to mislead anyone by depicting organizational issues as needing only minor adjustments. Inaccurate descriptions are often instructional and provide clues that can lead to the underlying problems. We find these clues by paying close attention to the process aspect of communication and determine the consistency of the process with the content that is verbalized.

The Solution

In this case, David stepped out of the traditional liaison role during the medical care coalition meeting and into the role of decision maker and spokesperson. David redefined the boundaries of his leadership role as a committee chairperson, relying on his vast experience and knowledge of the political process. He unilaterally carved out a policy position in the name of the Senior Campaign. Since we know something about David's background, we have some advantage in understanding his frame of reference and his motives. In addition, when the Senior Campaign refused to backpedal on David's public statements, the board tacitly supported David's statement of policy.

Jane's anger at David is understandable, but it would also be unfair to blame him entirely for all of the problems that ensued.

David's actions were within the framework of the organization's laissez-faire leadership style, reinforced over the course of many years. Furthermore, both Jane and Karen share some culpability by not orienting David to the norms of the organization. Norms can be a very powerful influence on an individual's performance as a volunteer or employee.

It is understandable that in the absence of clearly communicated norms and rules, the governmental affairs committee, under David's leadership, set its own direction and rules. When Jane challenged those rules, characterizing the policy position as "David's" and not "the Senior Campaign's," the members of the GAC perceived her statements as patronizing, unappreciative, critical, and a breach of their trust.

Interestingly, it was not David's comments that upset Karen and her executive committee but the perception of how the executive director managed the incident. In other words, they found fault with Jane's handling of the dilemma sparked by David's pronouncement.

First-Order or Second-Order Approach?

Given the history of role confusion at the Senior Campaign, it did not appear that any prior attempts had been made to clarify staff, board, and other volunteer roles and responsibilities. Without intervention, a pattern of behavior can establish itself and become dominant. By perpetuating such patterns of behavior, the nonprofit organization is locked into first-order mode. Specifically, an organization operates in first-order mode when activities of the organization adapt to the organizational environment and make either no change or slow incremental change to the organization's structure. Even if individuals or groups in the organization are involved in dysfunctional behaviors, the organization will remain in first-order mode until fundamental changes significantly alter the state of the organization.

Selecting Theories for Examining the Issues

The role confusion problems encountered in the Senior Campaign may be best understood by applying concepts that are embedded in the theories of conflict, relationship behaviors, and situational leadership, and exchange concepts of intergroup relationship behavior, groupthink, incongruent group norms, and escalation of commitment.

Intergroup relationship behavior occurs when two or more groups must work together to complete an assignment. By virtue of each group believing in their own set of norms and goals, intergroup behavior stimulates competition between the groups, as can occur between two committees, committees and the board, committees and management, board and management, staff and management, or the staff of different departments.

When groups compete, leadership styles tend to become autocratic. Members of a group not only tolerate a strong-fisted leader but also demand more loyalty to the group by its members. This profile resembles David's style of leadership and his committee's fierce loyalty.

A considerable amount of research has indicated that groups can place enormous pressure on individual members to conform to the group's standards and to express beliefs and attitudes that they would not otherwise have embraced. This may help explain the committee members' belief that David's actions were correct and responsible behavior. The committee members' belief in David is also telling. It suggests that they have passed through various stages of group development and achieved some measure of cohesion. Sharing a crisis as a group can often expedite the bonding process.

Jane and David independently behave in each of their roles according to their own set of assumptions about what is appropriate. Had they discussed their beliefs, they might have been able to reach some mutual understanding about each other's roles. Had this occurred, their ability to resolve conflict would have improved because they could discuss the events in the context of their understanding of each other's role. In the absence of such an exchange of ideas about roles and responsibilities, it is understandable that David would experience confusion about being rebuked for actions he considered appropriate. Likewise, the relationship struggles between Karen and Jane follow the same explanation of misguided assumptions and would explain Jane's confusion and feeling targeted for blame.

One of the presenting problems was related to recurring problems of volunteers acting independently. The real issue is not in the specific behaviors of the volunteers but that the Senior Campaign appears to be guided by a self-perpetuating force that no one can control. In this case, situational leadership studies would suggest that the Senior Campaign's leadership—specifically, the board chairperson, the executive committee, and the executive director— have not adapted their management or governance style to meet the motivational needs or level of directiveness for guiding the work of the volunteers and ensuring volunteer and organizational success.

Furthermore, the concept of groupthink may help explain the Senior Campaign's ability to continue, year after year, to present a strong and united public face or front. According to organizational behaviorist Joseph Champoux (2000, p. 190), groupthink is "a major dysfunction of cohesive decision-making groups." In the case of the Senior Campaign, groupthink is evidenced in the macroenvironment. On the macro level, we know that the Senior Campaign experienced recurrences of volunteers indiscriminately promoting policy positions that were never approved by the organization's board of directors. Rather than admit publicly to the mistakes of the organization, its leadership simply supports the policy positions put forward by volunteers. It is often easier for individuals, in or out of leadership positions, to quash their own doubts and misgivings than to confront a group member about his or her actions. Nonprofit organizations caught in this type of conundrum experience deficiencies in effective decision making and sacrifice the opportunities for corrective action. Consequently, by failing to prevent renegade committees and outspoken members from advancing their own agendas, the Senior Campaign became vulnerable to these recurring events.

Oddly, the Senior Campaign's reputation of being strong and independent is an unintended consequence of not backpedaling or retracting the unauthorized and controversial statements its volunteers have publicly made. To the outside world, the Campaign comes across as thoughtful, politically competent, and willing to take on the world for its beliefs. The publicity and reputation that the Senior Campaign enjoy are by-products of escalating commitments. The explanation of the concept of "escalation of commitment" is an organization's loyalty to decisions regardless of how flawed the decisions may be or how they were reached.

Formulating a Hypothesis to Guide Planned Change

Ideally, planning for an intervention should start with the presenting problems that were described by the nonprofit organization's representatives. If the intervention is going to be designed and implemented by someone internal to the organization, the target should also be the stated concerns that were voiced by members of the organization chosen to resolve the organization's issues. However, interventions are most effective when they not only address the presenting problems but also simultaneously target the underlying causes of those problems.

Some interventionists never fully disclose the blueprints that were developed to target the underlying issues of the nonprofit organization. The thinking behind this is that if the organization were ready to deal with these underlying issues, the presenting problem would have focused on the root and not the symptoms. This is the logic that psychotherapists use when an individual comes for therapy and states a presenting problem. The therapist may see that the complaint is really a symptom of a more complex problem. Many therapists proceed with therapy sessions focusing on the presenting problem because that is considered a safe zone for the individual, but the psychotherapist is simultaneously attempting to target the root of the presenting problem.

Whether the interventionist focuses on the presenting problem and also addresses it roots or chooses to detail the causes of the organizational dysfunction, which might cause embarrassment to some individuals, is neither intrinsically good nor bad. The choice of intervention is determined by which approach is most appropriate for the situation that led the organization to seek help.

In this case, the presenting concerns of the executive committee showed three areas in need of attention: the repeating issues of volunteers acting without sanction, wanting volunteers to have a satisfactory volunteer experience, and making a sound choice in the selection of a new executive director. I made an assumption that the underlying cause for these three presenting problems was role confusion.

Against this backdrop, the hypothesis would be that if we alleviate role ambiguity, the Senior Campaign would function effectively in all three areas of concern.

Devising an Alternative Intervention Strategy Based on the Hypothesis

Given the hypothesis, a first-order intervention would be to assemble some board and staff job descriptions and review them in a retreat setting or board meeting. These are necessary for any effective nonprofit organization, but using these tools alone will not transform an organization that is experiencing role confusion into a healthy and successful entity.

Instead, the second-order approach of our intervention plan started with the Senior Campaign's quest for a new executive director. The reason that this presenting problem was selected was because it holds the most possibilities to discuss a wide range of issues, including the underlying problems, in a nonthreatening way and without referencing specific people. This is an important consideration of any intervention plan. If a group is not at a point of readiness, directly discussing specific people and issues could cause certain individuals to feel embarrassed and singled out. The effect would likely close off discussion, and participation would drop off, leaving the intervention a failure.

The use of metaphor or storytelling is a powerful tool for discussing the most complicated and most difficult issues without having to discuss them in the first or second person. Metaphors provide us with a safe way to see and test organizational reality. Using this approach, we could discuss the traits of an ideal, "hypothetical" executive director for the Senior Campaign. In that context, we could creatively explore a variety of relationships and discuss what we think would be the ideal interaction between an executive director and the board, as well as committees, staff, and other stakeholder groups and individuals.

Because our discussions would be at the fantasy level, it is safe to propose all kinds of mechanisms, policies, and standards that could be devised to ensure that the vision of an ideal set of relationships has a chance of actualizing. Furthermore, we could discuss organizational structures that would support volunteers so they can be productive and feel satisfied and successful.

In the end, we have the basis for nonprofit organizational metamorphosis as a result of the key players of the Senior Campaign all sharing in a transformation of ideas of how their nonprofit organization could look and function. According to some of the leading organizational behavior experts, when an organization experiences metamorphosis, it can emerge "with a different configuration and strategic intent" (Hershey, Blanchard, and Johnson, 1996, p. 470).

Implement the New Strategy

I asked the executive committee to develop a list of all the organization's key stakeholders, volunteers, and staff. An invitation was sent to all of the members on the list, inviting them to a meeting at which they would have an opportunity to help shape the future of the Senior Campaign. The meeting, to be held on the grounds of a local botanical garden, was scheduled to last five hours, approximately one hour of which was set aside for breaks and lunch.

Forty-three individuals responded, including twelve members of the board of directors and five management staff members. Upon arrival, individuals were assigned to seats set up in a circle around the perimeter of the conference room. In the center of the room was a round table with eight chairs.

When everyone was assembled, those seated in the outer group were given a note pad and pen and were told that they were going to be observers for the day. They were asked to read through a statement of instructions and sign if they agreed to the processes that were outlined or else not participate and leave. The instructions outlined an agreement to remain silent while the meetings were in session. Observers were not to engage in discussion with other observers or shout out questions or comments. If observers could not remain silent, the instructions clearly indicated, they would be asked to leave the room. Should they be asked to leave, they would go to an adjacent room, where they could either tape-record their questions and comments or discuss them with an individual whose role it was to talk through the issues that excited the observers. Observers were also invited to step out of the room of their own accord and go next door to either record or discuss their issues.

The instructions were necessary to facilitate the process with as few disturbances as possible. Then, too, if someone had some relevant information to share, we wanted to capture it for later review. Furthermore, the purpose of having the observers sign the instructions and agree to the meeting rules was to ensure they understood the consequences of noncompliance. For some, being asked to leave the room could be a very embarrassing moment. On another level, the instructions were communicating an important message about structure, and they modeled a set of rules outlining expectations and adherence to one's role in the group.

The role of the outer circle observer group was to capture key statements they thought were important in considering a new director and the direction of the Senior Campaign. Also, they were asked to write down any words they heard that represented the sorts of values, knowledge, skills, and abilities they wanted in an executive director. They were also to identify words that represented the values and culture they would like to see reflected in the organization.

The group seated in the inner circle came to consist of three board members, one staff person, one volunteer. and three individuals from other stakeholder groups. They were not chosen at random; they were selected after the responses from the invitations had been collected. Based on my directions that we needed to identify individuals who were articulate, thoughtful, logical, reasonable, personable, not likely to get into confrontations with other participants if they disagreed, and truly caring about the future of the Senior Campaign, the executive committee made recommendations. Eventually, the list was paired down to the eight participants seated at the center table.

The eight were then paired off into four groups of two and were asked to take a stroll through the flower gardens while discussing the type of executive director that the Senior Campaign needed to lead them over the next decade. They were told that during their walks and the whole day they need not agree with each other or try to build any consensus. These additional instructions were given as a way of demonstrating that role differences can be discussed and that rules allowing for disagreements are indicators that disagreements are not only acceptable but expected.

After twenty minutes, the group reassembled. For the next hour, the eight engaged in a facilitated discussion based on the information that they shared with each other during their stroll. As much as observers may have wanted and tried to engage in the discussion or ask questions, they were not permitted. Anyone trying to violate the rules was asked to stop and capture his or her thoughts in writing. Any observers who felt the need to talk were directed to the tape recorder set up in the next room, where they could verbalize and preserve their questions or comments. Not only was this intended to be a very focused exercise, but it was also designed to model a clear separation of roles and adherence to the rules. The strict interpretation of the rules prevented role confusion among the participants.

For the rest of the day, members of the inner group were paired with different partners and focused on such matters as the type of director, the type of organizational environment that their ideal director would need to operate in, the roles of volunteers and outside stakeholders, and a review of the day.

The members of the observer group were asked to complete their written observations and return the next morning for a two-hour "debriefing." At the end of the debriefing, individuals were asked to volunteer to work in groups of three or four over the next two weeks. Assignments varied among the groups, but they were all asked to develop a plan for their assigned area. Assignments included work on the following questions:

- How do we ensure that volunteers are oriented to their roles and responsibilities?

- How can we ensure that they are satisfied and productive?

- How can we ensure that difference of opinion between the Campaign and any outside organization can be resolved in the best possible way?

- What questions should be used in interviews with prospective candidates for the executive director position?

For each plan, group members were also asked to develop a process map to show each step of their implementation scheme.

The Results

Over the next several months, each task force presented its plan and process map for review by the board of directors. During this time, the board was learning how to delegate assignments, adhere to rules, structure meetings and deadlines, and establish ground rules for meetings, decision making, and leadership. The development of the process maps gave them a new skill and the ability to ensure that there are processes for dealing with disagreements, conflict resolution, researching information, making policy decisions, and so on.

The people in charge of the Senior Campaign were ultimately able to successfully interview candidates because they knew the type of individual they were looking for. After they hired their new director, I was able to spend time with her to review the metamorphosis of the organization.

9

Financial Misfortune

The Problem

Astute money management is one of the most important skills a nonprofit manager can possess. This competency is vital to a nonprofit organization's fiscal health. When a nonprofit manager or board of directors reduces its focus on finances to a second tier of importance, it is a telltale sign that the organization is on the road to poor fiscal health. This condition can be characterized by bouncing checks, not paying bills, or double-paying vendors. The result of this situation includes becoming a bad credit risk, experiencing generalized panic about making payroll each pay period, and developing a poor reputation among lenders, banks, and funders. When a nonprofit organization is unaware of its true financial position and conducts its business as though there is enough money to pay all of its bills, there is a high likelihood that the outcome will be failure.

When nonprofit organizations experience financial misfortune, it is often a direct result of the organization's leaders' possessing limited knowledge and skill in the use of nonprofit financial management tools. Consequently, information that could be signaling a pending financial disaster may well go unnoticed.

Financial accountability does not just rest with nonprofit managers. In addition to their obvious legal fiduciary responsibilities, board members are expected to possess an understanding of how to read financial statements. Executive directors and board members who are financially astute are more likely to steer their nonprofit organization toward achieving effective outcomes. This means that in the process of making management or governance decisions, executive directors and board members know what to look for in financial reports. Their understanding of the reports enables them to raise appropriate questions, exercise fiscal accountability, and make prudent decisions about spending the organization's money.

A nonprofit manager needs skills far in excess of those of the nonprofit's board members. Executive directors are not expected to be as knowledgeable as accountants, but they are expected to have a strong working ability to develop and use organizational budgets. They are also expected to be able to read financial statements and know how to compare the organization's actual spending to the budgeted amounts for each fiscal year. Nonprofit managers are also expected to understand certain rules of sound financial management and ensure that the organization complies with all of its legal reporting responsibilities.

Executive directors and board members who are not financially accountable may be breaching their legal duties to protect and preserve the organization's tax-exempt status. Should the organization lose its tax-exempt status and jeopardize its ability to effectively function, it may be doomed to dissolution.

On a daily basis, nonprofit managers make decisions that are vital to the success of their programs. For this reason, all managers at every level in the nonprofit organization need to understand that there are financial ramifications to all of their programmatic and human resource decisions. According to Harrington Bryce (2000, p. 3), "Without money, no mission can be met or advanced in a market economy no matter how charitable or benevolent the mission may be." In order to ensure an adequate supply of money, nonprofit managers and board members must exercise their role in raising, earning, investing, and carefully spending money to achieve the organization's mission.

One puzzling but diagnostic question emerges from the following case study. Since it is common knowledge that board members have a fiduciary responsibility to their nonprofit organization, what would lead an active board of directors to avoid exploring its financial problems even when it has been informed that the organization may be on the brink of financial collapse?

The Case Study

The Council for Renewable Energy serves as a clearinghouse of information about the problems of nuclear energy and provides information about preferred alternative sources of new energy, such as solar and wind-generated power. Monies from various private foundation and government sources are used to educate consumers and encourage further research into renewable energy. To accomplish its programmatic objectives, the council subcontracts a majority of its funding to various nonprofit groups that specialize in energy-related matters.

Paul Busch is the executive director of the Council for Renewable Energy. Because Paul does not have an environmentalist background, he was a controversial choice. In fact, four of the twelve board members resigned over Paul's selection. The board's chair, Carla Bartlett, pushed very hard for Paul's candidacy, notwithstanding the threats of resignation from board members who had served since the organization's inception. Carla liked the idea of hiring someone with an M.B.A. degree who would bring a bottom-line orientation to the job.

Given the board's task of selecting its third executive director in five years and the fourth in the organization's ten-year history, Carla thought a new style of leadership was necessary. Despite the national reputation of the previous executive directors, the council had not flourished. At board meetings, the council's finance staff regularly reported that the organization was on the brink of bankruptcy. These doom-and-gloom reports went on for almost three years.

Paul met with the finance staff to review the organization's financial procedures. During this meeting, he discovered the root of the money problem. Three years earlier, one of the nonprofit organizations that does subcontract work for the council was having cash flow problems. It asked for permission to send a bill in advance of delivering services and get paid within three to five days of the beginning of the month. The payment plan was approved, and for consistency, all of the nonprofit's contractors were paid in this manner.

The contractors were understandably pleased to be paid in advance, but doing so caused a serious timing and cash flow issue for the council. Rather than follow recognized business practices, such as making payments fifteen to thirty days after services were delivered, the council paid all of its contractors thirty to forty-five days *before* it was necessary and weeks before the council received monies from various funding sources. By paying in this manner, the council would deplete its cash reserves and have to tap into its line of credit every month. Their reliance on the line of credit would continue until payments were received from the funders.

To fix this payment plan, Paul directed his finance staff to change the billing and payment scheme. Paul stated that the council would need to receive its funding in advance of paying for the contractor services. Moreover, contractors would not get paid until after the work was performed and no earlier than fifteen days after they had submitted a bill and the work was verified as having been performed satisfactorily.

The contractors were furious when they heard of Paul's plan, and several contacted their friends and professional colleagues on the council's board of directors. Consequently, the board ordered Paul not to change the financial billing and payment procedures. Paul voiced his concerns and asked for a reconsideration of their decision or he would have to resign.

Facing the potential loss of its relatively new executive director, the council asked me to facilitate an exploratory meeting between Paul and the executive committee of the board.

Analysis of the Case

Paul was fixated on the financial condition of the organization as the presenting problem. He knew that the council's cash flow problems occurred as a result of advance payments to contractors.

Lack of financial know-how was only part of the problem, according to Paul. He stated that the board had a responsibility to thoroughly investigate the cause of the organization's continued financial shortfall, and it had not done so. The council paid more attention to the status of its programs than to its administrative and structural responsibilities.

Certain residual issues remained unresolved following Paul's hiring. That he was hired meant that the majority of the board consented to the resignation of the four board members who would not relinquish their hard-line stance against Paul. They opposed his hiring because he did not have an environmental program background. Their threat to quit the board was their attempt to foil Paul's hiring, thereby maintaining the status quo and reinforcing the organization's programmatic direction.

When the contractors contacted the council's board members en masse, several board members wondered whether they had made the correct decision in hiring Paul. Some who were rethinking their position had felt guilty that they "betrayed" their former board colleagues who resigned under protest.

The Solution

In preparation for the meeting with Paul and the executive committee, I held some preliminary one-on-one meetings with Paul, the board chair, and a couple of other board members. I had learned that after Paul was hired, he reviewed all of the board minutes for the prior five years. He found that little attention was given to financial problems and just one acknowledgment that the organization would benefit from bringing in more grant awards. After he discussed the financial condition with key members of the

organization, it was Paul's opinion that the board treasurer, in addition to his own managers, was uncomfortable discussing the organization's financial condition.

Interviews also revealed that board meetings focused on committee and program reports and not on the organization's chronic
financial problems.

The composition of the board was homogeneous, with two-
thirds of the board consisting of representatives from other environmentalist organizations, and no member appeared to have a
strong financial background. Three board members were executive
directors of "grassroots" nonprofit organizations with budgets under
$100,000.

Some of the board members voiced their concern that Paul dealt
harshly with the contractors that they rely on for service delivery.
These board members were in favor of doing whatever was necessary to preserve their working relationships with the various environmental organizations serving as contractors, even if that meant
they would need to search for a new executive director.

Paul was unhappy with the culture of the organization and felt
as though he was in a "dysfunctional relationship."

First-Order or Second-Order Approach?

To Paul's credit, he saw a problem and went about investigating its
root cause. Paul viewed the organization's financial problems as a
(strictly first-order) cause-and-effect issue regarding financial management. Once he determined that the problem was tied to payment cycles, he made a decision on how to resolve it and
communicated the results to the contractors.

His problem-solving approach was also a first-order attempt at
change. Unfortunately for him, he met great resistance from the
contractors. Ultimately, his own board members would not back his
reorganization plan. Paul thought that his only way to save face and
reduce his frustration was to resign.

Selecting Theories for Examining the Issues

Paul is correct that the prior executive directors' and past and current board members' lack of knowledge and limited financial know-how were factors that contributed to the council's financial crisis. However, financial factors are just part of the problem. In other words, the finance issues, while real, are also symptoms of a larger and more complex organizational issue.

There are some clues that motivational and psychological reasons led to the organization's avoidance of these knotty issues. In reviewing the facts of this case, many issues surfaced when Paul was hired as executive director. We can comprehend those issues more clearly when using Lewin's Force Field Analysis theory. This theory can help us see why the council tried to resist hiring an executive director whose credentials were markedly different from those of previous executive directors. The selection of an executive director without programmatic expertise would be more than a symbolic change; it threatened the existing culture of the organization.

Selecting a manager instead of a program expert for the executive director position was a dramatic shift in organizational philosophy. For some board members, this change was too difficult to process and accept. Four board members threatened to quit as an attempt to prevent change from occurring and to restore homeostatic balance. Their viewpoint was that an executive director needed to have programmatic expertise, which Paul, the leading candidate, did not. Most of the board members, not just the four, thought it was counterintuitive to select someone who was not an expert in the focal areas of the organization.

Potentially, much stronger forces of restraint might have prevented Paul's hiring and deterred the impending change that his hiring represented. However, as a result of the board chair's strong command, some stalwart board members relinquished their attempt to keep things the same. The risk of change was mitigated by the board chair's promise that if Paul did not perform satisfactorily in the first six months, he would be terminated and she would step down as board chair. That was not just a powerful statement and endorsement (that satisfied all but the four veteran board members who had served since the organization was founded) but also a way for the board chair to strengthen her position of power, gain control, and rid herself of some competing forces, namely, the four board members. The fact that other board members conceded their view about the type of director they wanted bespeaks the influence the board chair has over them.

In addition to using Lewin's theory, the concepts of selective perception, filtering, and information overload may shed some additional light on the underlying issues.

The homogeneity of the group and its lack of comfort with financial matters contributed to the selective ignoring of the organization's financial condition by the board and management staff. According to organization behavior specialist Stephen Robbins (2002, p. 254), "Individuals shape their world through their perceptions. Once they have created this world, they resist changing it." So individuals are guilty of selectively processing information in order to keep their perceptions intact.

Assuming that Robbins is correct, we can see that the council's board and its former executive directors disregarded the magnitude of the organization's financial problems. They did so because to deal with the issue head-on would have distracted their focus from the environmental programs in the "safe" world they created. This is much like the "ignoring the elephant in the living room" phenomenon.

A second factor—information overload—also contributed to the council's distraction from its financial issues. The expression "information overload" is often used to describe the abundance of data (stimuli) that individuals receive on a daily basis from all sources—electronic mail, announcements, newspapers, television, billboards, faxes, along with input about the world picked up by the bodily senses.

Information overload is a powerful force that has been linked to stress resulting from either an inability to process or understand certain messages or a failure to process them at all due to selective screening of incoming stimuli. Information overload can have some serious consequences, as revealed in a 1996 Reuters Business Information survey of more than thirteen hundred managers around the world. The survey reported that 43 percent of the respondents suffered ill health, loss of job satisfaction, and deterioration of personal relationships as a result of information overload.

Information overload is analogous to what an individual might experience when visiting a foreign country and is unable to speak the language. No matter how much information local residents share with the visitor, the information will not be effectively processed because the visitor does not have the ability to process and comprehend the data that has been communicated. The experience can lead to feelings of stress, frustration, disorientation, and embarrassment. In the case of the council, the financial issues were like an incomprehensible foreign language to the board and its previous executive directors. Rather than becoming confused and stressed by trying to interpret and react to the financial data, it was easier for the board and managers to simply ignore the information. This defense mechanism kept the board and managers from becoming overwhelmed.

A third factor that contributed to the displacement of financial priorities by the board and previous directors can be explained using communication theory. Conceptually, there are two forms of filtering: intentional and unintentional. Intentional filtering is when a sender of a message deliberately distorts information so that the information that is conveyed is more palatable to the receiver. Filtering can be used to avoid delivering a harsh message, such as blaming someone directly for the organization's poor financial condition.

Avoidance of unpleasant information can occur on a continuum. At one end of the continuum, the sender of the message does not fully understand the issues and therefore does not convey messages accurately or downplays the importance of the message. At the other end, filtering can take place on an unconscious level of understanding to avoid conflict. The message can be filtered by the sender or by the receiver. In Paul's case, had he had a different personality, he might have succumbed to the pressures of his board's supportive actions for the contractors by filtering out his true emotional response of anger and frustration.

Formulating a Hypothesis to Guide Planned Change

Choosing Paul as its executive director represented a substantive change in the way the organization would function and approach decisions and policymaking. His hiring caused a redistribution of decision-making ability and altered power relationships that had long existed among the board members. In fact, the four individuals who were part of the founding of the organization and stood the most to lose in terms of power, influence, and decision-making control tried to leverage their loss by threatening to quit and then carried through on their threat. Interestingly, the departure of the four board members also benefited the power base of the board chair.

We should not lose sight of the fact that where a financial problem exists, the problem will not be solved until we first resolve the underlying conflict. Very simply, Paul likes exercising his authority and does not need to engage in consensus decision making. He is more of a loner and a quick decision maker in his business-oriented management style. The board members, by contrast, appear to be more communal in their outlook toward each other and their environmentalist contractors. Often individuals who are in close-knit groups look to their leader for guidance. This explains why the board chair was able to get support for Paul's hiring even at the loss of four board members.

These dynamics led us to formulate a hypothesis that suggested that two major pieces had to come together to resolve the human resource issues and the financial problem. One piece was to get Paul to confer with the board chair and his board before taking an action that makes sense to him. Because this group had a traditionalist out-look, Paul needed to use the power of their leader, the board chair, to get their approval.

The second piece was to get the board to give Paul a face-saving opportunity by recognizing him as someone who can operate independently. The board could do this by conveying that members see him as a highly intelligent and competent manager. Also, they needed to become very clear with Paul about their need to be involved in critical decisions and to be briefed by him and receive his "expert" recommendations before final action is taken.

Devising an Alternative Intervention Strategy Based on the Hypothesis

A second-order approach was designed to implement the hypothesis. I participated in the intervention, but if Paul or any members of the board had been knowledgeable about nonprofit organizational behavior and planned change, they could have created an intervention strategy to fit with the theories and hypothesis they would have formulated.

My first request was for Paul and the board chair to agree to a three-month exploratory period in order to see if Paul and the board could come to a resolution of their differences. I was cognizant of using humor as a deescalating strategy and described my role as being similar to that of a football coach. I would come up with a couple of different plays and ask members of the team to memorize the plays and implement them accordingly. Carrying through with the analogy, I told them that game day would be the monthly board meetings. Using board meetings as the context for change was important because this is where a board's collective decision making should be taking place. The purpose of asking for a three-month period was a way to get beyond the immediate period, which was emotionally laden with ill feelings and tension. Using a sports analogy was also a way of neutralizing the seriousness of the current struggle and transporting it to a different and less passionate milieu.

I helped Paul and the board chair outline a board meeting agenda. The agenda was a tool that would structure the roles of Paul, the board chair, and board members in a way that would bring together the two pieces referred to in the hypothesis.

The first item on the agenda fit with the board chair's influential powers. She would lay out some ground rules before the board meeting got under way. These were rather standard meeting rules. But it was not the rules that were important; it was reinforcing the board chair's control of the meeting that was most meaningful.

As part of his preparation for the meeting, Paul was asked to brief the board treasurer on the financial problems and make recommendations for resolving them. Paul was instructed not to ask questions of the treasurer or to make any reference to his earlier decision on payment changes that the board had nixed in response to complaints from contractors. The treasurer, for his part, had been told to ask as many questions as necessary in order to feel comfortable with his understanding of Paul's explanation and recommendations. The structure imposed on Paul and the treasurer was intended to model the type of relationship that they should have with regard to discussing and reporting on financial matters. The treasurer was asked to decide whether he or Paul would give the treasurer's report at the board meeting. Regardless of that decision, the treasurer was asked to make certain that he lay out an introduction to the issues before either deferring to Paul to complete the report or completing it himself. This was a way to reinforce the role of the treasurer while creating a cooperative atmosphere in the working relationship between the treasurer and the executive director.

The board was instructed not to make any immediate decisions in response to the treasurer's report and the executive director's recommendations. Instead, the board members were asked to use the remainder of the board meeting to outline questions that they would like answered before they would feel comfortable voting on any recommendation. They were asked to prioritize the questions

and identify the individuals and committees that should be addressing those specific questions and report to the full board at its next
meeting. Invariably, Paul's name was listed next to most questions.
This was an important acknowledgment of Paul's expertise. The fact
that the board was asked not to make an immediate decision was to
reinforce the idea that board members should explore and discuss
issues before reaching critical decisions. This was as much a message for Paul's benefit as it was for the board's.

The Results

At the second meeting, a more lighthearted atmosphere prevailed.
The meeting was structured along the same lines as the first meeting. By the third meeting, Paul and the board chair were working
more like a leadership team. The board treasurer asked for a motion
to adopt a payment plan that was along the lines of the plan that
Paul had wanted to implement. A major difference was that the
board indicated that it would hold a group meeting with the contractors to explain why the changes were to be made and to
announce a three-month period in which to phase in the new
billing cycle. It was suggested that the contractors each work with
Paul on this transition, and if they needed more time than three
months, they were to meet privately with Paul about that. The
board acknowledged Paul's ability to use his discretion in reaching
an arrangement with any contractor that was requesting additional
transition time.

The intervention addressed all of the elements of the hypothesis, including the most suitable acknowledgment and motivational
needs for Paul, the board chair, and a majority of board members.
This intervention also demonstrated that it was not necessary to
explain to Paul and the board the "why" of my instructions. Their
willingness to go along with the experiment and take directions
helped them transform the way they conducted council business.

I believe that they were able to deal with issues they previously avoided because they had a safe environment and a clear structure in which to operate. And they recognized that they could easily replicate the style of problem solving that was used during the first and second meetings.

10

Fundphobia

The Problem

Fundphobia is the fear of asking people to make financial contributions to a nonprofit organization. There are various degrees of reactions to the task of asking people for money, from mild discomfort to total panic.

People who engage in fundraising for a living will acknowledge that asking people for money is not an easy assignment, but more challenging is their task of getting organizational members to take an active role. For this purpose, professional fundraisers often rely on motivational techniques to obtain cooperation from board members and other staff. While board members understand that it takes money to fuel an organization, many resist their obligation to contribute and otherwise raise funds.

Like it or not, fundraising is a necessary activity of almost all nonprofit organizations. Most nonprofits do not have the luxury of being able to afford a full-time fundraising professional on staff who can design a campaign and provide support and guidance to board members and other volunteers. Instead of hiring a staff person, some nonprofits contract with a consultant or outside firm to provide fundraising support. Many other nonprofits elect to go it alone and simply rely on the skills of their executive director and the help of other staff and volunteers.

Regardless of who guides the resource development effort, authorities generally agree that the participation of the organization's board of directors is essential. Despite this widely held belief, some board members make use of one of two commonly applied excuses in order to avoid participation. The first excuse concerns the idea of developing and using a case statement, a strategic argument intended to elicit an emotional response that will lead an individual to part with money. Some board members say they will not participate in a blatant act of manipulation that is designed to make people uncomfortable so that they will give money to assuage their feelings of guilt. The second common excuse is a refusal to participate in soliciting funds because it is "like begging."

Furthermore, some board members who are less shy about participating in fundraising have difficulty soliciting funds from individuals who have recently made financial contributions or from personal friends. Their reluctance to approach recent donors is based on a feeling of embarrassment about continuing to ask for money as though the person were a patsy. As for not approaching friends, it may be the discomfort of discussing the topic of money. Some people feel there is a taboo about discussing money matters with close friends. Consequently, asking a friend to make a financial contribution feels like an invasion of personal privacy. Some also feel that asking friends, relatives, or neighbors to contribute money is "taking advantage" of their relationships because of an emotional bind that makes it difficult for them to say no.

Professional fundraisers have a different perspective on the act of asking people for money. They believe that the best prospects are individuals who already have demonstrated a commitment to the cause through prior contributions. Instead of looking at the act of fundraising as taking advantage of someone's goodness, fundraisers have adopted a reframed outlook on the activity of asking for money. They describe the activities of fundraising as a respectful four-step process:

1. Identifying a prospective giver

2. Cultivating the relationship

3. Presenting a stirring case about the nonprofit and its services

4. Inviting the person to make a financial gift

Whether it is a fact or a rationalization, some professional fundraisers claim that "inviting" people to make a financial gift gives them the chance to feel good about themselves. In other words, fundraising gives individuals the opportunity to be charitable and reap the emotional rewards through an eleemosynary act of giving.

Asking people for money seems like a simple task, but it is obviously not, given the unenthusiastic and avoidance behaviors of many board members, executive directors, other nonprofit managers, and volunteers. Why is it so difficult to get some board members to ask people to make financial gifts to advance a nonprofit mission the board member believes in? Why do some board members avoid making personal financial contributions to the nonprofit they volunteer for, even though they may contribute to other charitable causes when asked to do so?

The challenge is to find and remove the psychological barriers that impede board member involvement in soliciting money for or personally contributing money to the nonprofit organization.

The Case Study

Each summer for almost twenty years, children ranging in age from twelve to seventeen years old have been selected from choirs in Florida, Alabama, and Georgia to perform as the Tri-State Southern Children's Chorale. After a two-week music camp, the combined group travels around the southeastern states performing concerts for residents of nursing homes, hospitals, assisted living centers, and community-sponsored programs held in parks and auditoriums.

The Tri-State Southern Children's Chorale found itself in severe economic straits that had led to a series of staff layoffs. Although financial resources were potentially available from well-connected board members and at least three or more of the members have the personal wealth to simply write a check that would end the organization's financial distress, board fundraising is almost nonexistent.

Fewer than half of the board members have made financial contributions to the organization in the previous two years. In addition, four of the nine board members (including the chair) are senior executives from companies that have high visibility in the community as major sponsors of the local art museum, children's museum, symphony, and theater company. However, none of the four corporations has been a major sponsor of the Tri-State Chorale in the prior two years.

Admittedly, the organization was not in great fiscal health when Jeanne Martin took over as executive director three years ago, but there has been a steady decline during her tenure. The organization has managed to squeeze by on small grants from a culture tax, donations from audiences, membership fees from the families whose sons and daughters participate in the chorale, and checks from two board members to barely cover the balance of monthly operating expenses.

Despite the financial weakness of the organization, Jeanne and the board continue to plan performances and go about routine business. As a result, the general public is not aware of the organization's fiscal problems, which forced Jeanne and her staff to take cuts in pay and assume extra duties or face termination.

Making ends meet from month to month was becoming more difficult, and the staff was feeling the pressures and stress. After four months on the job, the organization's development director resigned in frustration immediately following a board meeting. She had asked the board to participate in fundraising by getting friends and colleagues to a series of special "Give Us a Hand" performances at which the audience would bid, as at an auction, on different songs, with the highest bidders selecting which songs the chorale would sing. The board's response was that a public appeal was "not acceptable."

Despite the development director's reminder that the board members had a responsibility to raise funds as well as make their own financial contributions to the chorale, they did not hasten to write personal checks or solicit any big gifts.

Jeanne resigned to take another job, and the chorale board hired an interim executive director, Suzanne Bertrom. Although Suzanne was a competent nonprofit manager, her recent arrival from the Midwest left her without close community ties that would help in jump-starting a fundraising effort.

Analysis of the Case

According to the e-mail that I received from Suzanne Bertrom, the Tri-State Southern Children's Chorale seemed destined to fold unless she could find a way to revitalize the organization and the board's giving efforts.

After meeting with Suzanne and the board chair to explore some of the history of the organization and receive a briefing on the developments of the past three years, I concluded that I needed a broader perspective on the organization. Arrangements were made for me to meet with some current and former board members and staff and some of the families whose children had participated in the program.

Meeting with the former development director enlightened me to the environment of the organization and also left me wondering about the decision by the board and the prior executive director not to follow the development director's revenue-generating ideas. Why did the board summarily dismiss the development director's advice?

I asked the board chair if he could explain why there had been such limited fundraising activity. The condensed version of his response was that there were three factions on the board. One group of five was adamantly opposed to fundraising personally and felt it was an activity that should be handled by the development director, executive director, and staff. The second faction of the board, which included the chair, consisted of four members who were interested in helping raise money but would not do so unless everyone on the board agreed to do an equal share of work and make individual commitments to raising a specified amount of money. The third faction was a subgroup of the second. Two wealthy board members agreed to provide just the minimum amount of money that was necessary to keep the organization afloat with a skeleton staff but would not provide a substantial gift to seed and grow the organization as long as other board members were not "doing their share" to actively help the chorale raise money.

The Solution

Despite suggested ideas for raising money, the board members chose not to move forward on any resource development program. They further refused to involve their corporate contacts and the companies that they worked for that had the capacity for giving in the community. And wealthy board members would not ask their friends for money.

Two members provided monthly checks to the chorale, limiting the size of their gifts to the amount necessary to keep the organization afloat but not to staff the chorale's programs. Even though board members were capable of providing substantial support to the chorale, there appeared to be no glory in being the sole major contributor.

Even as the board's lack of action was contributing to the stagnation of the organization, board members sought to preserve their own reputations. Consequently, board and staff refrained from informing the public that the organization was in need of financial help.

To maintain her professional integrity, the development director resigned when her best advice—that the board should work together to involve friends and colleagues to solve the financial problems—was dismissed out of hand. In her resignation letter, the development director insisted on notifying the board members in writing that they were shirking their board duties by not participating in fundraising efforts. Admonishing the board members had no discernible impact on them. The Tri-State Southern Children's Chorale appeared to be incapacitated by board members locked in a stalemate and unwilling to exercise their fundraising responsibilities.

First-Order or Second-Order Approach?

As critical as it is to raise money to survive, the more the issue of money was directly raised, the more the board pulled away from that responsibility—it was like a donkey's tug-of-war! The development director's efforts were of the first-order kind, and when her pleas for help were ignored, she engaged in "more of the same" behavior. For example, lecturing board members that they have a legal, fiduciary, moral, ethical, or any other type of responsibility to participate in fundraising is a first-order effort. If board members are not initially responsive to these important and well-known directives, continuing with this form of first-order dialogue will not only be ineffectual but also be interpreted by the board as haranguing. Unless people willingly choose to comply with a first-order request or participate as victims of the exercise of power and coercion, telling them that they have a responsibility to engage in certain activities will not necessarily make it happen.

After four months with the organization, it was evident to this development director that board members were not going to heed her advice. Unfortunately, the development director did not have the knowledge and skills to use second-order alternative approaches, and so she resigned. And her interim replacement was no more certain than she had been how to move the board in the proper direction.

Selecting Theories for Examining the Issues

To examine the issues more closely, I chose a multiple approach, making use of four theories and two major concepts. The four theories were culture, attitude, equity, and participation theory. The major concepts were "purpose plus limitations," which comes from participation and motivation theory, and "negative inequity," derived from equity theory.

Theories on organizational culture help us recognize the chorale as operationally dysfunctional. An organization's culture does not just reflect the attitudes of its management and staff alone; it also includes the attitudes and philosophy of its board of directors. An organization's culture is shaped by how it is managed and governed and by the values the organization holds and pursues. In the case of the chorale, the board members have not demonstrated a culture of commitment. They seem more focused on what they will *not* do, with no consideration of the consequences for the organization's mission.

In this culturally conflicted milieu, it is important that we recognize the attitude differences among these board members. The theory of attitudes suggests that there is a connection between people's perceptions of their world and their behavior in it. Chorale board members with a strong antifundraising attitude will not participate in fundraising. By understanding how attitude formation and attitude change occurs, we may be able to shift the attitudes about fundraising of one or more board members. If we can change their attitude, we may change their behavior and perhaps then through social pressure or cognitive dissonance be able to realign the behaviors of other members of the group.

Equity theory helps us understand the stalemating behavior of the chorale's board. Four board members who want to be helpful have decided not to do fundraising because the remaining five board members are refusing. Instead of the four proceeding on their own, equity theory explains their barriers to participation. For some historical reason that was never made clear in the interviews with past and current board members, this group will not engage in activities out of an inner belief that it would be unfair to work harder than the other board colleagues. This interpretation of unfairness is also known as negative inequity. Organizational behavior theorists suggest that the perception of inequity can cause internal stress and psychological discomfort. It can be a reason for a board member to withdraw from traditional fundraising roles and responsibilities.

What I thought was interesting was the fact that two board members helped keep the doors open by covering monthly short-falls. Given that this was a known fact to the other board members, they had no driving motivation to participate. According to participation and motivation theory (Barnard, 1938), individuals will participate at the minimum level to remain part of an organization. To increase the performance level of the chorale's board, it would require finding the right inducements that each member would experience as motivating. In addition, the concept of purpose plus limitations tells us that despite their noninvolvement with fundraising, these board members have a purpose in wanting to belong to the organization. It also helps us see that these board members have limitations that bar their participation in fundraising. The application of this concept further suggests the board's willingness to engage in fundraising is contingent on relationships with people who can help them achieve that purpose.

Generating a Hypothesis to Guide Planned Change

Given the purpose plus limitations concept, the hypothesis that I proposed was that board members will not respond to directives to engage in fundraising if they are experiencing limitations. It further suggests that if the board members who expressed a willingness to engage in fundraising would do so individually and offer to help or team up with one or more of the five holdouts, those five will likely agree to participate.

Devising an Alternative Intervention Strategy Based on the Hypothesis

We know that first-order problem resolution strategies have not worked successfully with this group of nine board members. We also know that the organization has not had any truly strong leadership from either the executive director or the board for several years. This is not a criticism but merely an observation that no one in a position of authority had been able to cut through the board deadlock; nor does it appear that anyone but the former development director had actually tried.

Without a doubt, good leadership is essential to the success of any organization. Good relationships between the executive director and the board and among the board members can also be essential to organizational success. Given all of these clues from the theories that helped us see what might be going on with this group, I toyed with two possible intervention strategies of the second-order kind.

Sometimes theories not only help us see the dynamics of organizational behavior in a way that helps us develop hypotheses for what is influencing the behavior of organizational members but also double as applied theories that help constitute our intervention strategy. In this case, one of the two approaches was based on leader–member exchange theory. This theory states that leaders categorize their followers into groups and tend to favor one group over others. In other words, leaders play favorites. The development of special relationships with members of the "in-group" can be crucial to the success of what a leader is attempting to achieve.

Research in this area suggests that favored members outperform nonfavored members of a larger group. Consequently, in-group members are more likely to work harder to satisfy the objectives established by the leaders. If the objectives of these leaders include participation in fundraising activities, in-group members are more likely to comply.

Another essential factor is trust. Higher levels of trust are the result of strong ties between people. The research on leadership suggests that leaders try to identify potential in-group members based on attitudes and personality characteristics that are similar to those of the leaders. This makes sense, seeing that trusting relationships are built on knowledge or predictability of how others think or act. The strategic decision associated with this model is to cultivate board relationships so that board members who are unwilling to engage in fundraising will want to become members of the in-group that has the knowledge, ability, and determination to raise funds for the organization.

The second possible approach was based on a behavioral leadership theory approach, in which the objective would be to shift the focus away from the "unpleasant" activities of fundraising and instead focus on the development of organizational plans consisting of goals and program objectives. In other words, the primary aim would be to reaffirm the vision and purpose for the Tri-State Southern Children's Chorale.

By (temporarily) eliminating the subject of fundraising from board meeting agendas and focusing only on the programs that each board member favored, the discussions would avoid the tension-filled topic of fundraising obligations. Instead, the board meeting agenda would list decision items involving the elimination, suspension, or paring back of programs because of the budgetary constraints. Reframing the problem as a budget decision issue and not a fundraising issue would be a more strategic and more subtle approach than hammering the board about responsibilities and obligations. There is a greater likelihood that by structuring the meetings and committee activities around discussions of program cuts, individual board members will look for ways to maintain their favored programs.

In implementing a plan like this, it is very important to resist the temptation to switch the focus back to "how can we fund it all without fundraising?" Instead, move closer to the issue of fundraising by asking board members to provide their advice and counsel on how to achieve their vision. The obstacle that the board will confront is the reality that their favored programs need funding. This will occur as a natural outgrowth of discussions that board members will not ignore. The overall objective would be for board members themselves, and not a manager or the board chair, to bring up the topic of needing more funds.

Implementing the New Strategy

Of the two second-order intervention strategies, I preferred the first but went with the second. I felt that the first approach, the implementation of the in-group strategy, would be more interesting and professionally challenging, and I would have used that approach if I were going to implement the plan directly. However, with my office some fifteen hundred miles away, logistics made that difficult. Because how long an intervention strategy will actually take is so unpredictable—especially if your hypothesis turns out to be incorrect and you needed to revise it—I knew that flying in to spend a week or weekend at a time might work to provide consultation but would not work with a model that requires more intensive supervision, constant analysis, and ongoing attention to the development of the working relationships among board members.

The interim executive director and the board chair worked cooperatively to implement the second approach, the one based on behavioral leadership theory, focusing on programmatic goals and avoiding discussions about fundraising. I provided some coaching over the phone to reinforce occasional face-to-face consultations. It is important to stress that if the executive director or the board chair had experience in alternative problem resolution approaches and planned change techniques, that person could have followed through without any outside assistance.

Suzanne and the board chair worked well together in shaping the board agenda and eliminating the topic of fundraising. Board members noticed the absence of the topic and indeed raised the question about its removal. The board chair replied that I had recommended that it be removed until some future date. It was important to give the board a straight answer to the question. It demonstrated that my consultation was leading in a direction to help them. Suzanne was also prepared and delivered the message, "Dr. Block said it was technical; it has something to do with his analysis of what fundraising approaches might be best for the chorale, and until that analysis is completed, we might find it more productive not to think about fundraising or discuss it."

This last message was very important to the implementation. Although board members could control whether they discussed the topic of fundraising or not, instructing them *not* to think about fundraising in fact forced them to think about it. Its absence from the agenda triggered thoughts about the topic, and shifting the pattern and content of communication at board meetings away from the topic also reinforced their awareness of its absence. In addition, they were told that I was working on this issue, and that would also lead them to think about it.

Part of the reframing was to shift how the board thought about fundraising and remove the matter as a target of contentious control and power. In the past, fundraising was a tool for arguing and dividing the board into factions and preventing discussions about vision and mission. By removing it from board meetings, board members had to shift their focus and concentrate more on program policy issues and the future direction of the organization. Instead of allowing fundraising to be used as a barrier, board members would individually have to sort through their ideas about fundraising and its place in the organization.

With the calendar on our side, Suzanne raised at a board meeting that the organization would soon need to develop a budget for its new fiscal year and recommended that given the chorale's financial constraints, the most prudent approach for the board to take in its review of the budget would be to use zero-based budgeting. This would force discussions about the justification to keep, revise, or eliminate every program offered by the Tri-State Southern Children's Chorale.

The Results

The zero-based budget discussions led the board to discuss the need for members to engage in fundraising. In good second-order form,

Suzanne reminded board members that I had recommended that they not discuss fundraising. Not to my surprise but to my satisfaction, the board members stated it was not my place to tell them what they should or should not be discussing. One member said it best: that it was the board's responsibility to figure out how to bring in the resources.

Several months later, a follow-up with the Tri-State Southern Children's Chorale revealed that the organization had been on track in raising money, had hired Suzanne on a full-time basis, and was negotiating a series of performances throughout the United States, sponsored by a number of major corporations.

11

Founder's Syndrome

The Problem

Nonprofit organizations are created to improve or protect some condition that exists in local, national, or worldwide communities that has an impact on humans, animals, or the environment. With few exceptions, all nonprofit organizations exist as a result of a vision of an individual or a group of individuals who were dedicated to accomplishing some specific end that could best be achieved through an organizational entity. Whereas many individuals have ideas about different ways to improve the human condition, safeguard the environment, and protect endangered species, relatively few individuals in the world are sufficiently determined to set up an organizational entity to translate their ideas into reality. Those who do establish nonprofit organizations as extensions of their personal visions and drive are known as "founders."

How is it that founders, to whom we are indebted for their efforts to improve our enjoyment of life, also wind up as the subject of our criticism and scorn? How is it that the inherent qualities of the individuals whom we honor for their leadership and vision are the same qualities that we later seek to suppress? What is intrinsically wrong with so many founders that their critics—and even their supporters—eventually come to object to their motivations and tactics—an organizational behavior pattern that has been dubbed "founder's syndrome"?

Founder's syndrome consists of the array of influential powers and privileges that are either exercised by or attributed to the founder of a nonprofit organization. The word *syndrome* suggests an undesirable or troublesome condition. Behaviors that are associated with founder's syndrome are considered problematic and often associated with heavy-handedness. Building consensus and balancing and sharing power are not the norm for founder behavior. Instead, founders tend to dominate and control the direction of the organization they started.

It should really be no surprise that individuals who found organizations want to control the destiny of those organizations. After all, founders start organizations with an aim to accomplish some specific mission, and they have an enormous personal stake in achieving their organizational goals. Would we think it improper for the founder of a for-profit company to use his or her position of leadership and privilege to influence the direction of board decisions or the work of the company's management and employees? I would guess that we would admire any corporate founder who is so tenacious and personally driven to fulfill the company's vision and destiny.

For some reason, we in the nonprofit sector expect founders of nonprofit organizations to act differently, adopting the role of genteel egalitarians who favor decision making by consensus and refrain from personally influencing decisions. Perhaps the distinction is consistent with the expectation that nonprofit organizations should not be keeping an eye on the bottom line of the balance sheet, as for-profit businesses are expected to do, but should instead be focusing on the mission of serving the public good.

Whether we agree or not, society does apply one set of value-based standards to for-profit corporations and their leaders and a different set of value-based standards to nonprofit organizations and the people responsible for running them. Consequently, there is a polemical, almost Marxist struggle as to whether we should be promoting the independent behaviors of a founder as though possessed of the spirit of a pioneer or reining in and training the founder to be less expansive or autocratic and more inclusive and democratic.

Unfortunately, this chapter will not resolve that philosophical struggle, which is a suitable topic for a book of its own. Instead, this chapter will acquaint you with some of the dynamic problems associated with founder's syndrome, such as examining how founders and nonfounding organizational members (such as staff, volunteers, and board members) engage in behaviors that tend to escalate problems. Alternatively, we will explore an approach to developing second-order interventions that will help these groups solve problems effectively, enabling them to get on with their mission-oriented activities and services.

The Case Study

I have selected two particular case studies to exemplify the dynamics of founder's syndrome. These two nonprofit organizations differ in mission, size, and the extent to which their founders have engaged in conflict with board and staff members. Despite their obvious organizational differences, these two case studies demonstrate that a *syndrome* is a cluster of behaviors, reactions, and thought processes, exhibited in this case to preserve one's organization and further one's self-interest as the organization's leader and key decision maker.

How founders actually comport themselves when feeling threatened and how they react to preserve their position of privilege and power will vary from case to case. In some situations, founder behavior is annoying but tolerable; in other situations, founder behavior disrupts the organization's ability to function. Our two case examples illustrate that spectrum of symptomatic behaviors. On one end, the founder behavior creates conflict and mild controversy among staff and board members. On the other end, the founder syndrome conflict engenders considerable organizational dysfunction.

Rafting on White Water, Inc.

Rafting on White Water (ROWW) is a twelve-year-old nonprofit organization that promotes the sport of river rafting on white water. ROWW was founded by Justin and Kristen Rogers. It started as a small informal club that eventually grew into an international membership organization featuring training programs, certification programs for river rafting guides, *White Water* magazine, a special insurance program for ROWW members, and a travel agency. ROWW also licenses the use of its name for specialized equipment and products, including rafts, life jackets, helmets, oars, sunblock, and protective clothing.

Justin serves as ROWW's executive director, and Kristen is its chief operating officer. The Rogerses' son, Jerome, was hired as vice president of marketing, and their daughter-in-law, Amanda, is vice president of human resources. As founder and incorporator, Justin lawfully handpicked the members of the first board of directors. Despite what appears to be a conflict of interest and would generally be looked at as suspiciously like nepotism, Justin appointed his son and daughter-in-law as voting members of the governing board along with his wife and himself. In addition, five non–family members accepted board positions.

After almost a dozen years, the board of directors experienced attrition, and Justin selected three new replacement board members. Unlike the old board members, the three new members did not have the same allegiance to Justin and were not inclined to simply go along with his recommendations. One new member, a banker, challenged the financial integrity of ROWW after discovering that Justin and Kristen were receiving salaries from all the related companies. Salary decisions were made without any input or approval from the past or current board. The new members did not want to be accused of any improprieties, such as allowing for self-dealing and excessive compensation. Under a cloud of liability, the two longtime board members joined with the three newer members to form a united front. They agreed that it was in everyone's best interest to evaluate the performance of their CEO, Justin Rogers, and to establish a salary and benefits package for him. The board thought it would be prudent to have it in the records that the board had made the determination following a performance review. Unsurprisingly, the other four board members—Justin, Kristin, Jerome, and Amanda—voiced strong disagreement.

Justin expressed anger that the board did not trust his judgment, and he adamantly refused to participate in any performance evaluation. He stated that it was an insult to him and part of a conspiracy to oust him so that the newcomers could run ROWW and benefit from a financially healthy nonprofit organization that he and his wife had created.

The board members tried to reason with Justin, claiming that they had legitimate concerns and needed to protect the organization and themselves. In protest, Justin, Kristen, Jerome, and Amanda walked out of the board meeting. As he was leaving, Justin announced that the board was not going to be able to make any binding or legal decisions because the bylaws specify that viable decisions can be made only when a quorum of two-thirds of the members is present at the time of a vote. The board would be two members short of a quorum.

Following the walkout, Justin arranged for a restraining order that barred the five board members from entry into the ROWW office building. The request for the restraining order stated that ROWW's 117 employees needed assurance of being safe from aggression and potential workplace violence.

Outraged by Justin's hostile actions, the board sent a certified letter terminating his employment. Justin's attorney replied that the board's letter was "retaliatory and blatant harassment" and that the board had violated its legal duty of care by meeting without proper notice and without a quorum.

The five board members found themselves in a quandary. They did not want to take any action that would sully the organization and risk its tax-exempt status. The five board members hired an attorney who filed legal briefs asking the court to recognize the five as the legitimate board of directors acting on behalf of its twenty-thousand dues-paying members. They asked the court to uphold the board's decision to terminate Justin Rogers, claiming that the Rogers family's participation constituted a conflict of interest and "self-dealing." They also argued that the Rogers family's protestations and their act of leaving the board meeting were interpreted by the remaining five board members as tantamount to a resignation of their posts.

Mountain Town, Inc.

Developments near Lake Dillon sprouted up wherever a private landowner or homeowner was willing to sell property. The former mining community of Dillon was transformed into a resort playground for skiers, weekend escapees, and tourists interested in an assortment of outdoor activities during the winter and summer months.

Jill Reynolds started Mountain Town after close friends were forced out of their rented apartment because it was being converted to condominiums and timeshares. Many of the longtime local residents were also forced to relocate as far away as thirty miles and had to commute back to Dillon for their jobs. Mountain Town's stated mission was "to ensure the availability of affordable housing."

Jill recruited five active volunteers and a board of eight members, all of them friends who had been homeowners and business owners long before the development boom began. Many of the local business owners were actually grateful for the new surge of development. It provided steady customers, and some owners were expanding their business operations for the first time in twenty years.

When Jill was forcibly removed from a county commissioner's meeting for being disruptive, it became clear to board members and

volunteers that Jill's agenda was more antidevelopment than pro-
ductively seeking affordable housing. Some members of the board
and the local chamber saw Jill's activities as an impediment to their
economic development goals. Furthermore, her protest demonstrations at various resorts both disturbed and upset many tourists who
had come for a relaxing experience and ended up leaving angry.

Jill persisted with her activities even after a majority of the board
members voted to prohibit further demonstrations by Mountain
Town. Not only did Jill defy the board's directives, but she also met
with various board members in private and threatened that if they
didn't resign, she would lead protests in front of and inside their
shops and in their neighborhood. She delivered the same message
to her volunteers and the paid staffers who wanted the organization
to focus on developing relationships with developers to build affordable housing. Some board members, volunteers, and staff did resign;
others stayed either because they believed in Jill's aim or out of fear
that if they were branded "anti-Jill," they would suffer some personal consequences.

Analysis of the Case

ROWW made no requests for organizational behavior intervention.
The conflict moved into the legal arena of a courtroom. A ROWW
board member who had read a research article I had written on
founder's syndrome contacted me. The board wanted to share the
details of its founder's syndrome experiences and sought my off-the-
record reaction!

With permission, I include the ROWW case in this book
because of the unusual degree of relationship collapse between the
founder and his board. Moreover, I also want to demonstrate that
there are similarities and common organizational behavior dynamics across all organizations experiencing founder syndrome problems, from the mildest to the most extreme. In other words, it
is important when first examining a presenting problem not to

overreact or underreact to the content of what you hear. You can hear the wildest and most tortuous of examples, but your reaction needs to be based on process, analysis, and observation. You will often find as you cut through these problematical situations that the symptoms and struggles have a commonality to them despite how grave the presenting problem first sounded.

In the Mountain Town case, the organization's primary funder contacted me and asked that I facilitate a conflict resolution meeting with Jill and her supporters and the Mountain Town stakeholders. The funder was not aware of the extent or nature of the conflict, only that there was discord between Jill and some board members. I became involved only on the basis that Jill and the board would consent to meet one time and then decide if I should return. My conditions also included that I would give the funder an account of the situation only with the permission of the Mountain Town organization and only after it had screened my report.

The Solution

Founders tend to be entrepreneurs; they are innovative people with ideas and a vision. The founders of ROWW and Mountain Town were innovative and motivated individuals. The two nonprofit organizations grew, although to different levels. Management skills, social skills, and organizational know-how were not factors in the formation of these two organizations.

In each situation, the board tried to limit the behavior of its founder. These efforts led to serious organizational and personal conflicts. In ROWW, Justin's lack of close ties with the newer board members made it difficult for him to influence their decisions. Consequently, they did not hesitate to question Justin's management decisions. His refusal to cooperate with the board, acting within its rightful duties, was a bold move but not uncharacteristic of founders. Clearly, Justin did not want the board of directors to contest his decisions about his compensation and the salaries of his wife, son, or daughter-in-law.

Justin's behavior became less rational and more defensive when he lost the capacity to control the board agenda and his ability to sway votes to his favor. Interestingly, Jill's response was similar when her board challenged and tried to regulate her activities. In her case, Jill made private but direct threats to board members, volunteers, and staff that if they didn't back off, she would make life uncomfortable for them.

Since the legal work of the board of directors officially takes place with a quorum assembled for a meeting, Justin's ability to restore his control and influence required that he sabotage the meeting by leaving it.

Jill also attempted to outmaneuver her board, but her method of gaining control was to use her power to threaten consequences if she did not gain cooperation.

Typical founder behavior is not that of a team player. In ROWW, Justin Rogers exhibited many founder syndrome behaviors in the form of his leadership and management style. His management and governance decisions went unchallenged until the composition of his initial board of directors changed. The three new board members had not been acculturated to the unwritten rules that reinforced founder behavior. Once Justin's privileges were opposed, the two remaining nonrelatives on the board felt free to join with the three new board members. Justin's customary founder behaviors became ineffectual once his leadership cracked under a severe challenge.

Jill's authority was also contested. Consequently, her behaviors escalated from routine founderlike behaviors to more radical behaviors. Jill's style may not have been as extreme as Justin's, but Justin had more in the way of salary and benefits at stake.

First-Order or Second-Order Approach?

Justin discovered that he could not gain control with his "normal" founder behaviors. Routine behaviors are considered a first-order effort. In this case, Justin's initial resistance to the board's suggestions of an evaluation was a first-order change effort. When this display of resistance did not get the reaction he was seeking, Justin's options were either to engage in more of the same first-order efforts or to react with greater intensity. By intensifying his response, Justin responded in a second-order manner.

Justin elevated his behaviors to a second-order approach, for example, when he led his relatives out of the board meeting, to leave the board without a quorum to conduct business. This unorthodox action for regaining control could be countered only by another second-order approach. In this case, the board's second-order approach relieved the five members of their decision-making responsibility and transferred it to the judicial system.

Jill's antidevelopment efforts at the county commissioner's meeting and with her board and staff were first-order efforts familiar to many nonviolent protesters. When her board tried to contain her founder behaviors, she elevated her reaction to the second order by using coercion and intimidation.

The funder's request that I meet with Jill and her board was a first-order conflict resolution effort approach.

Selecting Theories for Examining the Issues

Demanding and controlling behaviors may not be typical for nonfounders, but they are the cultural norm for nonprofit organizations that are led by founders.

For years, Justin operated by strongly exerting his authority—textbook founder behavior. This pattern of behavior kept his organization in harmony. Once Justin could not control the board and the direction of the organization in his usual way, organizational balance, also known as homeostasis or equilibrium, was tipped. Jill's leadership was also challenged when her board asked her to stop protesting development activities.

Applying Lewin's Force Field Analysis theory is helpful for putting Justin's and Jill's founder behavior into perspective. Escalation of the driving forces were required in Justin's and Jill's attempts to maintain authority and control. When routine founder behaviors did not work, as they had in the past, both executive directors needed to increase the driving forces. Increasing the driving forces was a necessary step for taking over or impeding the restraining forces that adversely affected their abilities to control and influence the direction of their organizations.

The restraining forces were so strong that it took extreme driving forces to counteract them. On a continuum of founder syndrome behaviors, Justin's and Jill's counteractions went to the outermost boundaries. To the observer, their behaviors appeared irrational. From their own perspectives, however, Jill and Justin may admit that their reactions were severe but within the scope of what they would consider normal and justifiable (founder) behavior.

An explanation from personality theory could provide a helpful framework for understanding founder issues. Specifically, McClelland's achievement motivation theory (1961) can be applied in these two cases to decipher the behaviors of ROWW's and Mountain Town's executive directors and to understand how the directors' compelling drive to achieve may account for their behavior (which is perceived as unacceptable). The theory describes individuals as having either high or low needs in three areas: achievement, power, and affiliation. By applying this theory, we can observe that both Justin and Jill have very high needs for achievement, very high needs for power, and very low needs for affiliation. This formulation of needs is very likely to be the driving force behind the behaviors routinely exhibited by founders.

Need for Achievement

Founders are not just ambitious people with boundless energy; they are individuals who have a high need for achievement. The personality characteristics that are associated with the need for achievement are probably shaped through socially acculturated behaviors and feedback. This theory suggests that the need for achievement is an acquired need and therefore can be learned.

Founders are risk takers who find ways to detour around obstacles that would get in the way of their success. They are driven for self-interested reasons rather than being motivated by incentives from individuals or other organizations. Individuals who have the need for achievement do like to receive feedback about their performance, but they are not easily persuaded to change their outlook.

Founders are often criticized for their independent style, being more concerned about personally achieving their organizational goals and objectives than about others achieving the same goals and objectives. This characteristic of taking control and not depending on others is a major factor in this theory, and it fits the profile of Justin and Jill. Their profile also matches McClelland's theory that entrepreneurs have high achievement needs.

Need for Power

The activities of both ROWW's and Mountain Town's executive directors and McClelland's description of individuals who have a high need for power neatly overlay each other. Very simply, the need to control others, to make an impact, and to be influential are stereotypical descriptions of founders. Not only is it a need for power, but it is also a need to influence the behaviors of other people. My own research (Block and Rosenberg, 2002) has revealed that founders are very influential in persuading board members to vote in specific ways. This drive to influence also gives further affirmation to the charges that some founders are totalitarian in their management approach. Some are not. McClelland (1961) makes the point that there are two styles of expressing the need for power. In the approach that McClelland believes is more effective, the individual (the founder) uses interpersonal skills to persuade others to agree to believe in his or her point of view. The less effective approach, and the one that Justin and Jill followed, promotes a win-lose effort. In this formula for expressing the need for power, the key ingredients include using personal dominance, exploitation, and if needed, aggression.

Need for Affiliation

Founders are more likely to have a low need for affiliation. Founder behavior, especially in the example of ROWW's and Mountain

Town's founders, does not point to behaviors that reflect high needs for affiliation, which would include the need for warm relationships and approval from other people. Individuals with high affiliation needs tend to want to work in teams. Team orientation does not appear to be an important factor for founders.

Given the stereotype of the authoritarian founder, it is interesting to note that when McClelland applied his achievement motivation theory to countries in the world, he found that a high need for power and a low need for affiliation were characteristic of more totalitarian countries.

Formulating a Hypothesis to Guide Planned Change

Unfortunately, because of the breech in trust between the executive director and his board members, the ROWW situation deteriorated into an ugly legal battle that left all parties depleted of energy and spirit. Hypothesis building was not necessary because reconciliation was not their objective.

Hypothetically, had ROWW's executive director and board members wanted to resolve their conflict, the technique of reframing might have been the choice tool to use to demonstrate that each side was attempting to accomplish similar ends. Instead of their behaviors being interpreted as malevolent, both groups would need to be reframed as not just deeply committed to ROWW but also overly involved to the point of obsession. Given that perspective, the ROWW board and Justin and his family might be able to accept each other's astounding behaviors as less pathological and more extreme. At least one of the major factions must have the inclination to alter its assumptions and beliefs about the conflict in order for the reframing to be successful.

In the case of Mountain Town, if the board of directors and selective volunteers and staff could be convinced that Jill's behaviors are appropriate for her personality type and that her overzealous actions could be interpreted as a compelling act of commitment and dedication, the board may be able to temper its criticism, not overreact, and see Jill's behaviors as more eccentric than harmful.

At the same time, if Jill were to see the board members' attempts at limiting her protests because of some fear of theirs and not a forfeiture of their commitment, Jill might see them as weak individuals but not as traitors to the cause. If someone communicated this reframed outlook to Jill, further escalation of the conflict would not be as likely.

Devising an Alternative Intervention Strategy Based on the Hypothesis

In the development of an intervention strategy, I think it is helpful to meet with some of the key players beforehand, preferably alone. Some organizational behaviorists, especially those who adhere more strictly to systems and group theory, would recommend meeting with all the key players in one large group. The belief is that by not separating the members of the group, you can more accurately assess the dynamics of the group, determine how the dysfunctional behaviors are triggered, who has the informal power, and who takes on the role as scapegoat.

I think the idea of meeting as a group is sound theoretically, but there is plenty of opportunity to examine the group when it eventually meets with you. I feel more comfortable initiating a course of action by meeting the key players on a one-on-one basis; it helps establish rapport. Also, individuals tend to want to align themselves with the person identified as the intervener. By meeting alone, an alliance of sorts develops between you and the other individuals. This quasi-relationship puts people at ease when the entire group meets. Individually, each participant may also believe he or she has a slight edge and is one-up on everyone else as a result of meeting with you.

Because of the tendency to blame others for organizational dysfunctions, it may help to begin by reframing the importance of everyone's involvement, including individuals whose behaviors were considered problematic. It is somewhat disarming to reframe the issue as a relationship problem by pointing out that their feelings are more about a personal disappointment than about an organizational issue: an individual they held in esteem has personally rejected them. Furthermore, it may help to show them that they have been focusing on the "wrong end" of the problem. Instead of focusing on what has happened, they should be focusing on what their behavior means.

The intervention should lead to restructuring the group's behavior so that the group reinvests in the organization. The attempt will be to recapture the excitement and commitment that everyone had to the organization in its earlier stages of development. In its earlier life cycle, Jill represented herself and the organization in a way that gave the group something to believe in. Her passion and founder behavior was acceptable to the group during that period. To be successful in the intervention, Jill will need to recapture some of her founder behavior that the group had accepted. Otherwise, Jill's behavior will continue to be radical as a way of achieving some counterbalance to the founder behavior power that she lost.

Implementing the New Strategy

When I first met with the Mountain Town board after conducting all of the individual meetings, we discussed some ground rules for the meeting, the major one being no personal verbal assaults on anyone. My goal was also to avoid any attempt to discuss how or why the group had become so fractious.

I started by asking the group to discuss the organization's history. This is generally a good place to start a meeting like this because it reminds all the participants that they have shared roots. It reinforces the idea that at some earlier period, they were able to work in concert with one another and not against one another.

Asking the group to discuss the organization's original purpose can lead us to a first-order question: Is the original purpose of Mountain Town, Inc., still relevant today? Not surprisingly, everyone agreed that the mission was still relevant. When nonprofit organizations are experiencing a crisis, asking the organization's key players to discuss the organization's vision and what they want to achieve for the community through their nonprofit organization brings some element of hope and possibility back to the group.

After the first half-day meeting, I announced to the members of the group that I thought they had demonstrated a real interest in resolving their organizational issues, but I did not think that all of them were quite ready to let go of their anger and willingly resolve their differences. I reminded them that discussing issues openly has its risks and that our exploration needs to be paced accordingly. They were told that moving too quickly might make some of them feel very vulnerable, and vulnerable people tend to become defensive and arm themselves through words or actions. When making these types of general pronouncements, group members will invariably wonder if you are talking about them. The purpose of delivering a message of this type was to cause the group to consider that recent behaviors by both Jill and other organizational members were the result of their feeling threatened and vulnerable. If the reframing is successful, board members, volunteers, and staff may consider Jill's founder behavior in a different light, one that humanizes her behaviors, even those that originally seemed troubling and unacceptable.

If you plan to state something that has a clinical aspect to it, such as, "people are not ready or may be too vulnerable," you must be certain of two things. First, anything you say must have a specific purpose in your intervention plan. And second, whatever the communication, you must believe in it. In other words, you can use content and metamessages as part of your intervention plan, but only use statements that you actually believe in. Otherwise, on some level of awareness, members of the group will pick up on your insincerity. If people think you are saying something to manipulate them or trick them into doing something, you will lose your credibility and will increase the likelihood of a failed intervention. You can use truthful statements in your planned change strategy to induce a reaction and movement in the direction that the group had expressed an interest in going, such as problem resolution. Some organizational behavior experts refer to these types of behavior-influencing statements as "paradoxical intention."

In this case, I thought I needed to challenge the members on the idea of readiness. This statement can be a powerful second-order technique. Most people want to prove that they are ready. Should you choose to use these techniques as a planned change intervention strategy, it would be wise to fully understand the concept of resistance to change. This subject is well covered in the organizational behavior literature.

My objective in using this specific statement about readiness was to facilitate a psychological and social shift that would encourage group members to coalesce in an attempt to prove that my assessment of them was incorrect.

Between the first meeting and the second, I again held private one-on-one sessions to get a reading on the level of interest and commitment individuals had for serving on the board and whether they would do so with Jill at the helm. Many individuals wanted to give Jill the benefit of the doubt, but some still could not see her in a legitimate leadership role. There were also some reasonable questions as to whether the larger community would view Jill as a leader or a troublemaker. Almost everyone made it a point to tell me that he or she was ready for change!

In my meeting with Jill, I told her that I thought her greatest challenge was one of credibility. As a founder of an organization that was based on the need for affordable housing, moving away from that "noble" focus to active antidevelopment activities was very confusing to people.

My advice to her was that if she wanted to focus on affordable housing, she would need to make a special demonstration of that decision. On the other hand, I told her that if she wanted to focus on antigrowth and antidevelopment activities, she should start a new nonprofit organization. I told her that she really did not have the right to redirect Mountain Town away from the purpose that was stated to the IRS when seeking tax-exempt status.

Jill decided that her true passion was in trying to help community members find affordable housing and make certain that there was a stock of affordable homes in the Dillon area. Had she said otherwise, I would have worked with her to withdraw from Mountain Town and encouraged her to develop a new nonprofit organization.

Since Jill indicated that she wanted to return to her roots, I told her that she had an opportunity to "refresh" her position and "renew" relationships with individuals who once really admired her leadership style. I told her that when I thought the time was right, she should engage in some "founder leadership" behaviors that would greatly surprise, if not pleasantly shock, the members of the board, volunteers, and staff members. I told her that it would not work well for me to lay out the specifics of that plan but that I would give her some general instructions and she would have to decide as to all the reasons why she should change.

There were two purposes in my message to Jill. One part of the message was to remind her of her capabilities. She had engaged in some remarkable activities when she first formed Mountain Town as a nonprofit organization, gathering community support and making progress with the mission. The second part of the message was that her transformation had to be a very personal one. If I gave her step-by-step instructions, it would not be coming from "her heart."

My instructions were of the second-order variety. I was not going to be very explicit, and thus Jill was forced to examine her own motives, limitations, and interests. By telling her that she would need to surprise and even shock the stakeholders, she was forced to think about every one of the individuals who were serving on the board and volunteering and working for the organization. If I had given her a first-order direction to think about everyone, it would not have been accomplished to the same depth and scope as this second-order approach.

I met two more times with the group as a whole, still raising questions about readiness. That elicited a couple of lectures from board members telling me that they were tired of my saying that, and they talked among themselves and could not find one person who was not ready! That response from the group was more than I could have hoped for. It demonstrated that interaction occurred away from the meeting place, a signal that the group was becoming cohesive and was ready for the next step in the planned change strategy. A couple of hours after the meeting, I called Jill and told her that we were ready to implement "the plan."

The Results

To everyone's surprise, in the next edition of the local weekly newspaper, appeared a full-page ad from Jill, headlined "A Letter to My Neighbors." The ad named and thanked everyone who at one time or another had served on the board, as a volunteer, or as an employee of Mountain Town. The big surprise was the next part of the letter, which listed all of the individuals and companies that Jill had had conflicts with. She stated her apologies for the manner in which she had expressed opposition and invited all of them to an open house to meet the "new and improved" Mountain Town organization and board of directors.

Jill certainly surpassed my expectations and did succeed in surprising a great many people. She gained more respect for Mountain Town and herself than she had beforehand.

The case almost ended there, but there was still some first-order work to complete with Jill and the board, such as developing a solid organizational structure, ensuring proper approaches to board governance matters, including effective and efficient meetings and reporting systems, among other routine nonprofit organizational activities. This transformation, from problem-causing founder's syndrome behavior to a more inclusive management style, took approximately ten months.

By the way, at last report, the judge in the ROWW case ordered the parties to engage in alternative dispute resolution. Consequently, a negotiated settlement was reached between the board of directors and ROWW's executive director. The terms of this legal settlement are confidential, but it appears that ROWW does have a new executive director, and none of the board members is named Rogers.

Conclusion: Managing Nonprofit Organizational Change

The focus of this book has been on the assessment and resolution of seven major problems familiar to many nonprofit organizations throughout the world. Case examples provided a context for exploring the major issues. The issues were examined by using various lenses (frameworks, paradigms, and theories) that would enable us to gain critical insight into persistent problems. Direction was also provided for selecting or designing meaningful intervention strategies of either a conventional or unconventional nature that would lead to change and increase the opportunity for the nonprofit organization to be effective in its mission.

Having a method for assessing organizational problems and for designing problem resolution strategies is essential for becoming and maintaining an effective nonprofit organization. Furthermore, it would be advantageous for the nonprofit organization to operate in a systematically designed supportive environment and not be operating in a reactive and crisis mode. Ideally, the nonprofit organization would be managed to meet strategic objectives in a planned way.

The various frameworks that were discussed for resolving organizational problems can also be used as tools for enhancing the day-to-day management of the nonprofit organization. When used for this purpose, executive directors, managers, and board members can arrive at an organizational development mind-set.

Organizational Development Mind-Set

Organizational development is generally thought of as applying concepts from the social and behavioral sciences with the purpose of managing change in an organization. To have an organizational development mind-set means to manage like a change agent. Successful change agents manage with an energetic commitment to achieving desired change. They use theories and models from the behavioral sciences to assess and diagnose the situation and decide on a course of action.

Some managers play the role of change agent on an occasional basis when reacting to some precipitous event. However, managing on a year-round, day-in and day-out basis with a change agent's mind-set can be an effective approach for an executive director and other leaders. Executive directors and senior managers who can cultivate an organizational development mind-set need the skills and repertoire of behavioral science theories to raise pertinent governance and management questions to ensure that the organization is mission-driven and resource-rich.

Change Agent

Change agents are the hands-on managers who are given the responsibility to facilitate organizational change by using their skills and expert knowledge of theories of organizational behavior and planned change; the role of board members is oversight in their governing role. As specialists in the managing of organizational change, these managers would understand when to focus on first-order or second-order change efforts. Moreover, change agents are strategic thinkers who consistently observe the internal and external environment in which the organization operates, identifying barriers that will get in the way of the organization's forward movement, and accordingly devise strategies to circumvent those barriers.

Three Paradigms for Forward Progress

Successful nonprofit organizations are managed and governed with organizational visions and strategic goals as targets for organizational growth and future direction. For a nonprofit organization to experience the trajectory of forward progress in the direction of the organization's mission and vision, a course of organizational change is inevitable. Executive directors and managers need to prepare their staff for these changes, and the executive director needs to brief his or her board on the implications of impending organizational change.

Executive directors, senior managers, and board members each play a specialized role in the oversight of their nonprofit organization's achievements. As these characters each observe their organization and engage in dialogue to assess the organization's progress, their viewpoints, suggestions, recommendations, and directives will be colored by paradigms that shape beliefs about organizational movement, growth, and change. The framework may be based on an evolutionary paradigm, a revolutionary paradigm, or a learning organization paradigm (Champoux, 2000; Senge, 1990).

Individuals who see their organization through an evolutionary paradigm will tend to make decisions that are consistent with their belief that organizational changes occur incrementally. Managers and board members are responsible for advancing and supporting small incremental changes in phases over a period of time. In this framework, change occurs in a sequence with a beginning, middle, and end. The beginning stage is an identification period. In this early stage, managers and board members recognize that certain strategic decisions will need to be made to move the nonprofit organization toward its mission and vision. The middle stage is the implementation of assignments that are selected to advance the organization. Once the organization experiences forward progress, the managers and board members will attempt to reinforce the integration of those changes and bring stability to the organization. However, although this progression appears to move in logical stages, it may not always move smoothly. In reality, attempts at maneuvering an organization in a forward direction can be thwarted, forcing managers and board members to reexamine their decisions and the contextual environment. If necessary, the managers or board members may decide that the organization should backtrack to one of its former stages.

On the one hand, managers and board members who operate from a revolutionary paradigm will provoke more organizational stress as a result of the radical shift in strategic direction this paradigm represents. Of course, organizational stress can take a toll on employees. On the other hand, managing change by using organizational equilibrium as a jumping-off point might excite managers, staff, board members, and other volunteers who especially thrive on adrenaline-triggering pressure. Unlike the drawn-out incremental style of evolutionary decision makers, revolutionary change agents shift the organization's direction with one extraordinary major event. This management style requires strong executive director leadership that can convey confidence in the decisions and garner followership among managers, board members, staff, and external stakeholders.

The third model that some managers use as a framework for making decisions to advance their organization is the paradigm of a learning organization. Learning organizations have a culture characterized by risk taking. Managers are inclined to promote cross-department support, encourage dialogue, and allow for debate, disagreement, and the resolution of conflict and other problems. An objective for management is to decrease overall staff and departmental competition and to encourage collaboration.

Achieving the goals of a learning organization is not an easy assignment. While certain aspects of information sharing, collaboration, and some degree of risk taking are achievable objectives, some elements are much harder to attain. One characteristic of a learning organization is reducing the levels of management, known as "flattening" the organization's hierarchy. Trying to flatten an organization's structure and encourage functional conflict, for instance, are counterintuitive to the organizational processes to which most employees have been acculturated in this country. As long as there is an identifiable boss, supervisor, or other manager who has more authority than others, hierarchy will exist in an organization, and we should not pretend that it does not exist. To flatten an organization on paper, as illustrated by a management chart, is more of an illusory effect than a psychological reduction in power and influence. In addition, most people are taught to avoid conflict in the workplace and would feel uncomfortable being open and confrontational on the pretext that it will lead to a healthier organization.

Moving Forward

Reliance on nonprofit organizations is not waning. Nonprofit organizations play absolutely crucial roles in sustaining vibrant and caring communities. However, with the upsurge in the number of nonprofit organizations, the competition for resources continues to mount. More and more nonprofit organizations will face critical challenges for human and financial resources. If they are to survive in their communities, nonprofit organizations cannot afford to run inefficiently.

Successful nonprofit organizations will be those that have the capacity to change in response to changing environments and political winds. They require executive directors, managers, and board members who are responsive and who are not afraid to take bold steps to solve their organizational problems. The uses of organizational behavior theories are valuable tools to help us understand our nonprofit organizational problems and take advantage of problem-solving opportunities.

As Pogo once said, "We are surrounded by insurmountable opportunity."

Resource A

A Review of Organizational Behavior Theories

Each of the seven theories discussed in this Resource has been helpful in improving my understanding of organizational behavior and for designing planned change efforts aimed at enhancing overall nonprofit organization effectiveness. Throughout this book, one or more of these theories were used to demonstrate their utility as tools for change and for creative problem solving.

Some theories are stronger or better suited as an aid to understanding organizational behavior. One may be helpful for, say, problem-solving efforts, or you may find utility in some combination.

Each theory can be thought of as a special lens or framework for viewing nonprofit organizational problems. Although I discuss only seven of my favorites, the number of potentially helpful and functional theories is vast. In addition to using one of the seven to help me understand organizational issues in a multilevel way, in practice I may add additional theories into the mix to help crystallize my thinking about a problem that I am attempting to solve.

Behavioral Leadership Theory

Leadership is an essential concept of organizational behavior. The challenge associated with the concept of leadership lies in its definition. Leadership may convey different things to different people.

The proof of that is the voluminous literature on leadership found in several professional disciplines, including psychology, sociology, anthropology, and management.

Some of the conceptual arguments are very interesting. For example, does leadership differ from management? If leadership is a process of influencing followers, is any form of influence acceptable? Or is leadership persuasion the result solely of *noncoercive* influence?

The concept of leadership is crucial to understanding and analyzing nonprofit organizational issues and to developing strategies that can be used to solve organizational behavior problems that hamper the success of nonprofit organizations. For these reasons, it is important to recognize that a variety of individuals may be referred to as a "leader" in a nonprofit organization even if they do not fit various textbook definitions. Take, for example, the founder of a nonprofit organization. Is the founder a leader because he or she had the vision to start an organization to address an issue of his or her concern? Or are founders considered leaders until they engage in founder syndrome behavior, which is perceived as demanding and controlling?

For our purposes, it is less important to determine whether someone is genuinely a leader than to recognize how the interactional behaviors of a person who has been labeled a leader actually affect the organization's staff, volunteers, and clients. To simplify the matter, the terms *leader* and *leadership* in this book apply to executive directors, senior managers, and board members and the roles they play.

In the mid-1940s, researchers at the University of Michigan started a series of research experiments aimed at two categories of leadership behavior (Cartwright and Zander, 1960). One pattern of behavior was humanistic in its approach because of its employee orientation. The second category examined leader behaviors that focused on the output of employee production. Rensis Likert (1961, 1967) was influenced by the University of Michigan findings and took an interest in investigating management behavior patterns.

Likert, like several other management theorists, wanted to determine what type or style of management and leadership behavior would produce the best outcomes. Likert discovered that the most productive employees were supervised by individuals who focused on the human aspects of their employees' problems. These same supervisors also tried to build effective work groups. In contrast, supervisors who put pressure on their employees had the least productive employees.

Likert's conclusions about productivity were similar to some of the results of the Hawthorne illumination studies of the 1920s and 1930s. Among the research findings from experiments at the Western Electric Company's Hawthorne Plant, Elton Mayo (1933) and his associates (Roethlisberger and Dickson, 1939) found that increased worker productivity was the result of being supervised by managers who took a human interest in their employees. Similarly, Likert's research findings indicated the importance of placing trust in employees and demonstrating respect for their knowledge and skills. He found that it was necessary to inform experienced employees only about the objectives that needed to be accomplished and not dictate how to do the job. High productivity resulted from this form of generalized guidance. Low productivity was more common when experienced employees were closely supervised and given specific directions on how to do their job.

Likert placed these management style differences on a continuum. At one end, which he labeled System 1, was a highly structured, authoritarian style of management that is similar in description to McGregor's Theory X assumptions (1960). According to these assumptions, individuals are not interested in independent responsibility. At the other end of Likert's continuum was System 4, a management style based on trust, confidence, and mutual respect similar in description to McGregor's Theory Y assumptions. According to these assumptions, managers assume that their employees can be creative and self-directed if properly motivated.

The two remaining categories neatly fit in between Systems 1 and 4. System 2 could be characterized as a condescending management approach and a step up from System 1. System 3 is a step below System 4 and is characterized by management's having substantial confidence in its employees but not complete trust in all situations.

The University of Michigan studies and Likert's research were part of a series of investigations over a period of two decades that sought to differentiate the behavior patterns of leaders and their effects on employee satisfaction and production. More recently, some theorists have questioned the limitations of research that looks at leadership behavior on a continuum that focuses only on two categories: employee satisfaction at one end and employee production at the other.

The critics argue that new leadership-style models should be developed that are based on entrepreneurial concepts, such as risk taking and purposeful organizational change efforts. Whether the theories of earlier eras should be revised may become an ongoing tautological debate. The age of the theory should not be an important factor if we can extract critical lessons from its application. Whether we look to leadership models that emphasize two, three, or more categories of behavior will really depend on our understanding of the various theories, our interpretations of our observations of leadership styles, and the types of influences the behaviors of leaders have on others.

The leadership models and theories that were developed over several generations affirms that researchers can systematically observe and differentiate the behavior of individuals we call "leaders." Furthermore, it is helpful to know that it is also possible to observe and examine the impact that leadership behaviors can have on individuals affiliated with nonprofit organizations. By being able to recognize and sort the types of behaviors and their effects on nonprofit organizations, managers have enhanced opportunities to develop strategies that might counterbalance behaviors that are considered problematic.

Some behavioral leadership theories suggest that individuals can become more adept at being leaders if they are flexible in their leader style and demonstrate a caring response toward employees. Related theories suggest that the organization should assign leaders with certain management dispositions to supervise employees who would benefit from those specific supervision styles. Altering one's style of leadership or matching leaders to certain situations are among the management approaches that are classified as contingency models of leadership (Fielder, 1967; Hersey, Blanchard, and Johnson, 1996). The concept of flexibility is important in a contingency approach because some employees prefer a more definitive understanding of the organization's direction and the role they play in it. Alternatively, some employees are content with simply focusing on their work products and do not have a desire to know the "big picture." As for work style preferences, some employees want very little supervisory guidance with their work assignments. Others prefer detailed instructions so that they know exactly what their supervisor wants from them on a day-to-day basis. Whether behavioral leadership theories are used to focus our understanding on the leadership role of executive directors, senior managers, or board members or on the supervisory preferences of employees and volunteers, in its application we should be mindful that we are also observing behaviors that are influenced by each individual's personality traits (Bennis and Nanus, 1985; Bennis, 1989).

Personality Theory

An individual's personality will have some bearing on the behaviors and attitudes the individual brings to the nonprofit organizational role he or she fills. Because personality traits are so vital to understanding the behavior of individuals, interest in the subject of personality has exploded in recent years. This upsurge of interest has moved personality from the scientific to more commonplace or pop psychology applications. In fact, examining the influence of personality characteristics in the workplace is no longer the exclusive domain of organizational behavior specialists.

Personality typecasting has become a popular activity in organizations. Many human resource departments have new hires complete one of several available questionnaires that categorize individuals by personality type, such as the Myers-Briggs Type Indicator, the LEAD, the Managerial Grid, or the BrainMap. These various classifying tools inform individuals what their predominate style or preferred patterns of interaction would be in the workplace.

With knowledge of one's own personality profile and the profiles of other employees or volunteers, a manager can alter his or her naturally preferred style of interaction in order to maximize the supervisory relationship. Personality profiling can also be used for enhancing peer-to-peer interaction. When colleagues have an understanding of each other's personality types, they can learn to anticipate their peers' behaviors and statements. Furthermore, organizations that emphasize team-oriented work groups could have an advantage in completing their work assignments through an understanding of each team member's interaction patterns or styles. Equipped with this knowledge, team members have the advantage of listening to their teammates more intently and with greater clarity. Similarly, individuals can learn to communicate words and images to their teammates in a manner that improves information sharing. Team members can also choose to overlook certain offensive response styles from team members because they know that their teammate's behavior is personality-driven rather than a response to something they may have done.

There are many different classifications of personality. A personality type represents a class of behaviors that some individuals have in common with other individuals who act or behave in similar ways in similar circumstances. These distinctive combinations of behavior have become known as a personality type. For example, a class of manipulative behaviors has been classified as the "Machiavellian" personality type. Individuals who constantly work, are competitive, and have difficulty relaxing and engaging in leisure activities are said to have a "Type A" personality.

Many different combinations of personality attributes exist. Some personality attributes are learned, and some are innate. In the field of organizational behavior and psychology, an abundance of literature suggests agreement among a large number of researchers that the human personality can be described along five separate dimensions that underlie all personality types: agreeableness, conscientiousness, emotional stability, extroversion, and openness to experience. On each of these dimensions, an individual can fall anywhere on a continuum from high to low.

Agreeableness: An individual labeled high on agreeableness would tend to be more cooperative and trusting. An individual rated low on agreeableness would be expected to be more focused on himself or herself and less interested in the work of others.

Conscientiousness: An individual who is low on the continuum of conscientiousness would not be particularly careful in on-the-job performance. A person high in conscientiousness would be very organized and efficient.

Emotional stability: An individual on the high side of emotional stability would withstand stress better than a person rated lower on the continuum. Individuals who score lower on the scale of emotional stability may have self-esteem issues and lack confidence in their work performance and their abilities.

Extroversion: An individual who is low on the extroversion continuum would come across as shy, not particularly sociable, and quiet. A person rated high in extroversion would be friendly, open, and relationship-oriented.

Openness to experience: An individual who is high in openness to experience tends to have an artistic edge and a creative imagination. Individuals lower on the scale of openness to experience prefer more familiarity and are less curious than their more open counterparts.

Maslow's hierarchy of needs (1954) and Herzberg's two-factor theory (Herzberg, Mausner, and Snyderman, 1959), based on hygiene factors and motivators, are well-known theoretical models that have been used over the years to explain the driving forces of human behavior in organizations. A lesser-known theory, but one that is based on empirical research, is McClelland's achievement motivation theory (1961). Like many of the personality theories that can be used as a lens to examine the potent forces that drive human behavior in nonprofit organizations, achievement motivation theory can be used for that purpose. It can also be used as a framework for viewing and solving organizational behavior problems. This theory, developed a half-century ago at Harvard University, suggests that individuals with a high need for achievement differentiate themselves from other individuals. They are driven to excel and to personally succeed at their goals rather than take on a task simply for material rewards.

In addition to examining the need for achievement, McClelland also considered the implications on human behavior of an individual's need for power and the need for affiliation. The theoretical model considers an individual's behaviors in an organization in the context of having either high or low needs or motives in each of these need categories (achievement, power, and affiliation). The individual who has a high need for achievement may be a high achiever and an entrepreneur but does not necessarily have the social skills or inclination to be a supportive and effective manager. A person with a high need for power is driven to control others and wants to be recognized as an influential and indispensable player in an organization. An individual who has a high need for affiliation would generally be characterized as people-oriented and a consensus builder. Individual behavior is influenced by the predominance of a need or by some combination of high and low needs.

Expectancy Theory

Expectancy theory is based on individualized perceptions of need (Vroom, 1964) and can be differentiated from other motivational theories that tend to generalize more globally about the needs that drive human behavior, including such popular theories as Maslow's hierarchy of needs and Herzberg's two-factor theory.

There are three essential phases to expectancy theory. In the first phase, the individual is confronted with a task. In response, the individual assesses his or her own abilities to perform the task. An individual who concludes that he or she has the requisite skills or knowledge to perform the task may then accept the assignment. Before making any final determination to move forward on attempting the task, however, the individual shifts into the second phase of the theory, in which the individual assigns some level of probability that he or she will be able to complete the task and achieve success within a given time frame.

The strength of the assigned probability is related to the individual's experiences and a belief in the adequacy of his or her knowledge and skills. The third phase of expectancy theory occurs if the individual believes that he or she can successfully perform the task with reasonable effort. In this final phase, the individual determines the likelihood of receiving a personally valued reward if the task is successfully achieved.

Overall, the theory is built on a sequential ordering of three interactive relationships. The first relationship is *effort leading to performance*, based on the belief that performance will result from exerting a reasonable effort. The second relationship is based on *performance leading to rewards*, in which the attainment of a desired reward is the result of accomplishing at a certain level of performance. The third relationship is premised on *rewards leading to personal goals* as personal goals or needs are realized by receiving a reward from the organization. Therefore, the theory posits, if individuals carry out their organizational responsibilities as they had predicted and obtain the reward that leads to personal satisfaction, there will be a propensity to undertake similar tasks in the future. When the three relationships are actuated, individuals exert greater efforts in their organizational activities. On the other hand, if they do not receive the level of personal recognition that they had anticipated, it is unlikely that they will attempt similar types of assignments for that organization.

Expectancy theory can be used as a tool to help explain the level of effort and performance of a board member of a nonprofit organization. Board members will actively fulfill their governance obligations if they believe that their participatory efforts will lead to some personally desired outcome. Expectancy theory would also explain two reasons for the absence or limitations of board member participation. First, a board member operates from a deficit position when he or she does not know the requirements of his or her board role. This eliminates the opportunity to personally bring about a psychological connection between fulfilling board member expectations and receiving intrinsic or extrinsic rewards. Second, a board member may know what is expected but may believe that putting forth a great deal of effort will not yield the preferred reward. Consequently, the person may either limit his or her performance or choose not to perform at all.

In addition to aiding in the explanation of board members' level of efforts of participation, the theory can be used by executive directors as a tool for designing opportunities that can foster board members' interests and increase their involvement with the nonprofit organization. To successfully use expectancy theory as a motivational tool, the executive director needs to be an astute listener and a keen observer of individual behavior. By listening to what board members say before, during, and after meetings; observing board member interaction; and learning about board members' personal backgrounds, employment, family life, and personal interests, the executive director can hypothesize about the type of performance-reward relationships that would be suitable for each individual board member.

An executive director who understands that an individual's interests and values evolve over time will not rely on a single episode to design an intervention strategy using an expectancy framework. Since the identification of board members' motivational factors needs to be updated on a regular basis, the executive director must have the conceptual ability to consider and analyze many variables simultaneously. Given the opportunity, the executive director would facilitate the involvement of a board member with a specific task that would benefit the nonprofit organization. The executive director could, for example, ask a board member to help review a marketing plan, write an article for the organization's newsletter, or accompany the executive director to a meeting with a high-powered foundation director. The executive director can also make committee assignment recommendations to the board chair and encourage action on those recommendations. To come up with the right match, individual differences must be taken into account because people have differential needs. With this key in mind, the executive director will draw on conceptual elements of effort, performance, and reward satisfaction. By selecting the elements that will have personalized meaning for the individual board member, the executive director creates a link between a worthwhile task, the board member's performance abilities, and an appropriately meaningful reward.

Lewin's Force Field Analysis Theory

Kurt Lewin (1947) developed an organizational development theory that could be used as an analytical and planning tool for determining where the emphasis of a change effort should be directed.

Influenced by the field of physics, Lewin's Force Field Analysis suggests that there are competing forces that influence the target of a change effort. In Lewin's theory, the manager has major decision choices. One choice is to focus efforts on leaving things as they are, maintaining the status quo.

Another option is for the manager to introduce change efforts by increasing the driving forces that direct behavior away from the status quo. Driving forces tend to move in the direction of change. These forces can be fueled by positive energy that comes from recognition, productivity, and other achievements. A manager may also have to make decisions about responding to forces that impede organizational change. Forces that thwart or reduce change efforts are restraining forces. These negative forces may be the result of unhappy workers, a poor working environment, or unfair labor practices, among other negative situations.

At times organizations are like two individuals on a seesaw that is suspended in midair. This seesaw stalemate or equilibrium is a balance between the driving and restraining forces. Depending on what the manager wants to achieve, a decision can be made to tip the balance or to maintain the equilibrium. After tipping the balance to create a successful change effort, a manager would likely want to reestablish equilibrium in order to reinforce and stabilize the change. This would require new strategies to balance the driving and restraining forces.

Consider an organization whose board chair is the founder of the organization. Because of the board chair's domineering behaviors and the lack of teamwork that his directives foster, the staff and several board members have decided that they are victims of founder's syndrome (see Chapter Eleven).

After an informal lunch meeting to "welcome" their newly hired executive director, two factions of board members communicated their desires to her. One group cautiously discussed its organizational concerns and gave warning to the new executive director, telling her that if she wanted to keep her job, she should be careful not to exert too much independence from the wishes of the board chair. This advice represented restraining forces intended to maintain organizational equilibrium.

The members of the other group informed the new executive director that they appreciated the former executive director's efforts at trying to change the power structure of the organization. Although the former executive director was fired as a result of his efforts, these board members were sponsoring driving forces aimed at generating change.

Communication Theory

The ability to express a message verbally and to listen to and interpret what others say is a crucial management skill. Effective managers must be able to communicate about the need for change and describe the processes that they want staff to follow. Without these skills, a manager can stand in the way of organizational change efforts. The challenges experienced by managers are intrinsic to using a language in which words can be misunderstood. Because talking is such a common activity, most people do not reflect on the complications that can occur through speech. However, communicating a message is far more complicated than it seems because people assign meaning to the words they hear, react to the tone of voice and body language of the speaker, and look for consistency between the speaker's verbal and nonverbal behaviors. Consequently, a manager's style of communication can have an effect on the results of problem-solving and organizational change efforts.

Watzlawick, Beavin, and Jackson (1967) suggest that the nuances of human communication can cause systemic interaction problems that are characterized as personal or relationship confusion. Confusion can occur when a person speaks because individuals communicate not one but two messages simultaneously: a verbal message and a relational message. A verbal message is content-oriented and provides meaning through the information it conveys.

A relational message, sent at the same time, qualifies the original message through nonverbal means—tone of voice, for example, which can come across as anything from angry to jovial. Relational messages can also be conveyed through physical behaviors, such as smiling or frowning, crying or laughing, or through body posture that communicates interest in or detachment from the discussion.

Modifications of voice and behavior can produce perceptual alterations. As exemplified by the work of behaviorist Ivan Pavlov more than a century ago, we know that the mechanics of how words are interpreted can lead to certain actions. The results of Pavlov's work went beyond the common understanding that dogs can be conditioned to salivate in reaction to the ringing of dinner bells. Pavlov's conditioning experiments demonstrated the symbolic nature of human behavior. He found that human actions are often in response to the meaning that a listener gives to the words that he or she hears.

Whether a message is constructed in writing or is conveyed through the spoken word, the individual acting as change agent or problem solver would benefit from knowing how to convey a message in the most effective manner to his or her audience. In other words, a communicator could influence, encourage, or prevent certain behaviors if the communicator knows what words or conveyed meaning would trigger the desired response (a conditioned response) from his or her listeners.

Applying this information, one nonprofit human service organization discovered that words and language could have important representations and meaning in its public relations efforts. Consequently, the managers decided not to use a generic newsletter but instead to produce four separate specialized newsletters, one directed to clients, one to funders, one to other organizations in the field, and one to in-house staff.

The decision to produce four newsletters was made because management realized that each stakeholder group interprets messages from its own perspective. With that awareness, the managers now make certain that the messages in the newsletters are tailored to their intended audiences. For example, professional jargon is banished from the client newsletter. Language is used to convey a confident organization with expertise in certain areas of specialization. Photos are used to help convey the message. By contrast, no photos are used in the newsletter that goes out to organizations in the same field. In these, professional jargon is used to convey the image of a knowledgeable, state-of-the-art member of the sector.

In the newsletter addressed to current, former, and potential funders, the articles, documenting the organization's many good works, are intended to portray the organization as a fundworthy entity with a track record of cost-effectiveness and success. Articles also include statements of thanks and recognition to funders and volunteers. The staff newsletter focuses on staff accomplishments, staff activities, announcements of staff promotions, information about career opportunities, advice on reducing workplace stress, offers of continuing education programs that are sponsored by the organization, and highlights of the organization's benefits.

The newsletters are used not only as a tool to help convey information but also to define the nature of the relationship between the sender and each receiver group. The specialized newsletters also serve to shape and reinforce the organization's supportive culture.

Whether or not we are aware of it, our selective methods of communication are used to define human relationships. Consequently, human communication systems convey not just content and relational messages but also some emotional element that defines the relationship between the message sender and receiver. Consider the experience of sitting on a bus, train, or airplane. When you sense that the person seated next to you wants to strike up a conversation, you can wordlessly communicate your willingness or unwillingness to engage in a discussion. For example, closing your magazine and inclining your head or smiling at the person would suggest an interest in being friendly. Remaining fixated on your magazine would send the opposite message. Although words may not be exchanged, the message of acceptance or rejection is communicated quite clearly.

Although the idea of sending a message to another person seems like a simple process, it is probably one of the most complex forms of interaction in which we engage. For some reason, messages can become distorted or interpreted incorrectly. The party game of telephone, in which a message is whispered from one person to another around a circle until it reaches the person who originated it, demonstrates how easy it is for a message to be unintentionally distorted.

Furthermore, the assignment of meaning that individuals give to words is another complex process that can lead to semantic problems and misunderstanding. A benign or even complimentary statement can be misinterpreted by the receiver of the message as a statement of criticism or ridicule. The subtleties that help us assign meaning to the words we hear are not taught to us. We learn through observation, trial and error, and participation in message sending and receiving.

The assignment of meaning to words is also a function of one's upbringing, personality, and cultural background. However, in a work setting, we may not be in a position to determine the personality traits of the individuals with whom we attempt to send and receive messages. Also, we may not be in a position to ask others to explain the cultural nuances in how they sent or received and interpreted a message.

Individuals sometimes construe negative motives and intentions based on communication from different frames of reference. I recall on two occasions asking employees to come to my office to discuss a matter when they inferred that they were going to be fired. On both occasions, I had intended to offer them a promotion! Apparently, being invited into the boss's office can produce a state of anxiety that leads individuals to assign to the communication a motive or intention that truly does not exist.

Given all of the possible places and ways that a message can be distorted, there is a very good reason why most people state that "poor communication" is the major reason for conflict in their interpersonal or business lives. From all of this, we can deduce that to effectively manage and govern a nonprofit organization, an individual requires not only knowledge of management principles but also the skill and ability to use judgment and examine messages. By learning how to scrutinize messages, managers and board members will improve their opportunities for organizational success.

Intergroup Conflict Theory

Unless individuals in an organization have participated in interdepartmental or board-and-staff training, it is highly unlikely that individuals from one departmental group will have an orientation to the tasks or know what is important to members of other departmental groups. Dissimilarity of values and diverse goals and objectives among groups can affect how members of one group interact with members of another group even though they all work or volunteer for the same organization and are guided by one organizational mission statement.

These interactional or process differences between group members can spark conflict between groups. The social and psychological forces that spur intergroup conflict are analogous to how Democrats and Republicans relate to each other's different positions on public policy issues, even though they are "all for America." Conflict is also a result of a form of competition that can occur when department members, board members, committee members, or any special grouping of individuals develop ties to their own subgroup's norms and goals and lose sight of where their subgroup fits into the bigger picture of the nonprofit organization and its mission.

Decision-Making Theory

If you ask someone to describe the process he or she follows to make a decision, the person is likely to say, "I don't know," or else describe a rational decision-making model. The process of rational decision making is the common problem-solving model reviewed in college psychology and communication courses. Although some variations of the model exists, it basically follows six sequential steps:

1. Define the problem.
2. Identify the important ingredients of the situation and what is important to the decision maker.
3. Weigh the pros and cons.
4. Determine if alternative solutions exist.
5. Prioritize the solutions.
6. Select the decision choice, based on the likelihood of achieving the results.

In reality, most management and governance decisions are not made with careful scrutiny or in so precise a way as following six logical steps. Instead, most decisions are made intuitively, heuristically, or emotionally. Intuitively formed decisions are based on a reservoir of prior experiences and learned information. Heuristically formed decisions are based on events or information stored in one's recent memory. Emotionally formed decision making does not draw on facts. In this mode, decisions are impulsively reached in reaction to feelings of stress or any emotion or combination of emotions from feeling happy to feeling very angry. When reaching emotionally formed decisions, individuals also engage in decision strategies that are influenced by failed or problematic decisions made in the past.

Resource B

Recommended Reading

Atkinson, J. W., and Raynor, J. O. *Motivation and Achievement*. Washington, D.C.: Winston, 1974.

Barrick, M. R., and Mount, M. K. "The Big Five Personality Dimensions and Job Performance: A Meta-Analysis." *Personnel Psychology*, 1991, *44*, 1–26.

Beach, L. R. *Making the Right Decision: Organizational Culture, Vision, and Planning*. Upper Saddle River, N.J.: Prentice Hall, 1993.

Blake, R. R., Shepard, H. A., and Mouton, J. S. *Managing Intergroup Conflict in Industry*. Houston, Texas: Gulf, 1964.

Block, P. *Stewardship: Choosing Service over Self-Interest*. San Francisco: Berrett-Koehler, 1996.

Block, S. R. *Perfect Nonprofit Boards: Myths, Paradoxes, and Paradigms*. New York: Simon & Schuster, 1998.

Bobocel, D. R., and Meyer, J. P. "Escalating Commitment to a Failing Course of Action: Separating the Roles of Choice and Justification." *Journal of Applied Psychology*, 1994, *79*, 360–364.

Bunker, D. R., and Wijnberg, M. H. *Supervision and Performance: Managing Professional Work in Human Service Organizations*. San Francisco: Jossey-Bass, 1988.

Conger, J. A., Kanungo, R. N., and Associates. *Charismatic Leadership*. San Francisco: Jossey-Bass, 1988.

Deal, T. E., and Kennedy, A. A. "Culture: A New Look Through Old Lenses." *Journal of Applied Behavioral Science*, 1983, *19*, 498–505.

Denison, D. R. *Corporate Culture and Organizational Effectiveness*. New York: Wiley, 1990.

Drory, A., and Romm, T. "The Definition of Organizational Politics: A Review." *Human Relations*, 1990, *43*, 1133–1155.

Farrell, D., and Petersen, J. C. "Patterns of Political Behavior in Organizations." *Academy of Management Review*, 1982, *7*, 403–412.

Herman, R. E. *Keeping Good People*. Winchester, Va.: Oakhill Press, 1999.

Herman, R. E., and Gioia, J. L. *How to Become an Employer of Choice*. Winchester, Va.: Oakhill Press, 2000.

Kline, P., and Saunders, B. *Ten Steps to a Learning Organization*. (2nd ed.) Arlington, Va.: Great Ocean, 1993.

Kuhn, T. S. *The Structure of Scientific Revolutions*. (2nd ed.) Chicago: University of Chicago Press, 1974.

Leckey, A. *The Lack of Money Is the Root of All Evil*. Upper Saddle River, N.J.: Prentice Hall, 2000.

Lewin, K. *Field Theory in Social Science*. New York: HarperCollins, 1951.

Marshall, E. M. *Transforming the Way We Work: The Power of the Collaborative Workplace*. New York: AMACOM, 1995.

Mohrman, S. A., Cohen, S. G., and Mohrman, A. M., Jr. *Team-Based Organizations*. San Francisco: Jossey-Bass, 1995.

Nutt, P. C. *Making Tough Decisions: Tactics for Improving Managerial Decision Making*. San Francisco: Jossey-Bass, 1989.

Schein, E. H. *Process Consultation: Its Role in Organization Development*. Boston: Addison-Wesley, 1969.

Schein, E. H. "The Role of the Founder in Creating Organizational Culture." *Organizational Dynamics*, 1983, *12*, 13–28.

Schein, E. H. *Organizational Culture and Leadership*. San Francisco: Jossey-Bass, 1985.

Schindler, P. L., and Thomas, C. C. "The Structure of Interpersonal Trust in the Workplace." *Psychological Reports*, 1993, *73*, 563–574.

Sherif, M., Harvey, O. J., White, B. J., Hood, W. R., and Sherif, C. *Intergroup Conflict and Cooperation: The Robbers Cave Experiment*. Norman, Okla.: Book Exchange, 1961.

Thompson, J. G. *Organizations in Action*. New York: McGraw-Hill, 1967.

Widmer, C. "Why Board Members Participate." In R. D. Herman and J. Van Til (eds.), *Nonprofit Boards of Directors: Analyses and Applications*. New Brunswick, N.J.: Transaction, 1989.

References

Argyris, C., and Schön, D. A. *Organizational Learning II*. Boston: Addison-Wesley, 1995.

Ashby, W. R. *An Introduction to Cybernetics*. London: Chapman & Hall, 1956.

Barnard, C. *Functions of the Executive*. Cambridge, Mass.: Harvard University Press, 1938.

Bennis, W. *On Becoming a Leader*. Boston: Addison-Wesley, 1989.

Bennis, W., and Nanus, B. *Leaders: The Strategies for Taking Charge*. New York: HarperCollins, 1985.

Block, P. *The Empowered Manager: Positive Political Skills at Work*. San Francisco: Jossey-Bass, 1987.

Block, S. R., and Rosenberg, S. "Toward an Understanding of Founder's Syndrome: An Assessment of Power and Privilege Among Founders of Nonprofit Organizations." *Nonprofit Management and Leadership*, 2002, *12*, 353–368.

Bolman, L. G., and Deal, T. E. *Reframing Organizations: Artistry, Choice, and Leadership*. (2nd ed.) San Francisco: Jossey-Bass, 1997.

Brill, P. L., and Worth, R. *The Four Levers of Corporate Change*. New York: AMACOM, 1997.

Bryce, H. J. *Financial and Strategic Management for Nonprofit Organizations*. (3rd ed.) San Francisco: Jossey-Bass, 2000.

Cartwright, D., and Zander, A. (eds.). *Group Dynamics: Research and Theory*. (2nd ed.) New York: HarperCollins, 1960.

Champoux, J. E. *Organizational Behavior: Essential Tenets for a New Millennium*. Cincinnati: South-Western, 2000.

Drucker, P. F. "What Business Can Learn from Nonprofits." *Harvard Business Review*, July-August 1989, pp. 88–93.

Fielder, F. E. A *Theory of Leadership Effectiveness*. New York: McGraw-Hill, 1967.

French, J., and Raven, B. "The Bases of Social Power." In D. Cartwright (ed.), *Studies in Social Power*. Ann Arbor, Mich.: Institute for Social Research, 1959.

Hersey, P., Blanchard, K. H., and Johnson, D. E. *Management of Organizational Behavior: Leading Human Resources*. (7th ed.) Upper Saddle River, N.J.: Prentice Hall, 1996.

Herzberg, F., Mausner, F., and Snyderman, B. *The Motivation to Work*. New York: Wiley, 1959.

Kilmann, R. H. *Managing Beyond the Quick Fix*. San Francisco: Jossey-Bass, 1989.

Lewin, K. "Frontiers in Group Dynamics: Concept, Method, and Reality in Social Science; Social Equilibria, and Social Change." *Human Relations*, June 1947, pp. 5–41.

Likert, R. *New Patterns of Management*. New York: McGraw-Hill, 1961.

Likert, R. *The Human Organization*. New York: McGraw-Hill, 1967.

Maslow, A. *Motivation and Personality*. New York: HarperCollins, 1954.

Mayo, E. *The Human Problems of an Industrialized Civilization*. Old Tappan, N.J.: Macmillan, 1933.

McClelland, D. C. *The Achieving Society*. New York: Van Nostrand Reinhold, 1961.

McGregor, D. *The Human Side of Enterprise*. New York: McGraw-Hill, 1960.

Nigel, H. "The Theory of Metagames." *General Systems*, 1966, *11*, 167–186.

O'Connell, B. *The Board Member's Book: Making a Difference in Voluntary Organizations*. New York: Foundation Center, 1985.

Ott, J. S. *The Nature of the Nonprofit Sector*. Boulder, Colo.: Westview Press, 2001.

Reuters Business Information and Benchmark Research. *Dying for Information? An Investigation into the Effects of Information Overload in the UK and Worldwide*. London: Reuters, 1996.

Robbins, S. P. *Organizational Behavior: Concepts, Controversies, Applications*. Upper Saddle River, N.J.: Prentice Hall, 1998.

Robbins, S. P. *Essentials of Organizational Behavior*. (7th ed.) Upper Saddle River, N.J.: Prentice Hall, 2002.

Roethlisberger, F. J., and Dickson, W. J. *Management and the Worker*. Cambridge, Mass.: Harvard University Press, 1939.

Senge, P. M. *The Fifth Discipline*. New York: Doubleday, 1990.

Taylor, B. E., Chait, R. P., and Holland, T. P. "The New Work of the Nonprofit Board." *Harvard Business Review*, September-October 1996, pp. 36–46.

Vroom, V. H. *Work and Motivation*. New York: Wiley, 1964.

Watzlawick, P., Beavin, J. H., and Jackson, D. D. *Pragmatics of Human Communication: A Study of Interactional Patterns, Pathologies, and Paradoxes.* New York: Norton, 1967.

Watzlawick, P., Weakland, J. H., Fisch, R., and Erickson, M. H. *Change Principles of Problem Formation and Problem Resolution.* New York: Norton, 1974.

Index